Essays on Adolf Loos

Christopher Long

Contents

Adolf Loos, 1930. Adolf Loos Archiv, Albertina, Vienna.

Preface

The essays in this book span roughly the last decade and a half. I wrote the first of them, on Adolf Loos's book *Trotzdem*, in 2002; the most recent essay, "Becoming Loos," I first completed in 2017 and revised in the late spring of 2018. I wrote each piece separately, in most instances in response to a request from an editor or a museum curator. I did not set out to forge a complete view of Loos, his work, or his import, but to seize upon moments or themes that seemed to me illuminating. Rereading the essays now, I am struck that they do have some coherence – beyond the fact that they cover most of Loos's lifetime. All of them, in one form or fashion, are essentially about Loos's thought. Although I remain deeply interested in Loos as an architect (he was the author of at least a dozen buildings and projects that are truly great), and I have written about his architectonic work at some length, what I find most compelling about him is his power and uniqueness as a thinker. What is indeed so arresting about Loos – almost from his first days in New York, as I seek to demonstrate in "Becoming Loos" – is his ability to perceive and understand the realities of modern life with a luminous clarity. Loos, almost but not quite alone among his contemporaries (one might think here above all of Le Corbusier), was gifted with the capacity to see beyond the moment, beyond what was ephemeral and superficial. He understood from the outset that the problem of modernism was not the problem of style, but the problem of understanding how the world was changing. What was central for him was to discern how to respond to those changes. Loos's reading of the situation of his day was at times economic and political; from quite early on, he was a Socialist in outlook and sympathy. But, even more, what drove his thought was a belief that the crisis of the new age was inherently cultural. The inner forms of daily life, whether shaped by the introduction of new modes of production or new materials, whether affected by new technologies or expertise, whether altered by profound economic or social change, were fundamentally a cultural issue. If one concern drove Loos throughout his active career as architect and writer, it was simply, "How should one comport oneself in the modern age?" Which is to say, "How should one dress?" "How should one eat?" "How should one find joy and repose?" And, above all, "How should one dwell?"

The answer to these questions, Loos was sure, had to do with grasping "where the culture was" – to discern what was truly modern, and what merely had its appearance but not its content. That seemingly simple idea is the fountainhead of Loos's entire critical mission. What he repeatedly assails in his writings is that which he perceives as sham: an aesthetic professing to be modern, and designers who contrived the new without necessarily grasping the true nature of modern culture. It was pretense, more than anything else, that was the target of Loos's ire.

Discerning the state of the culture was a manifold undertaking for Loos. He wanted to seize hold of a picture of modern Western culture writ large – to detect its innermost workings and where it was headed. But he also knew that what genuinely mattered was what the individual or the family believed and experienced. Modernism, in Loos's mind, was personal; it was bound up with the rituals of one's daily life. It was about everything we do: eating, sleeping, dressing, walking, finding pleasure and relaxation – in a word, *living*. To the extent that one can say that Loos is a great architect and thinker, it is because he was so absorbed with – and so responsive to – the small moments of everyday life. If his own sometimes idiosyncratic ideas miss the mark – he was fond of saying that modern, cultured people should not spend time gazing out of windows, for example – more often than not he hits the target dead-on. The domicile, he insisted, is first and foremost about comfort, not appearance. It is a refuge from the privations of the workaday world; it is about an attachment to place and the past, where nostalgia can still have free reign (which is one of the reasons Loos admits older objects into his interiors). An object, in the same way, draws its substance and meaning from how we interact with it. A chair, thus, is about how one sits well. That is the function of a chair, after all, Loos reminds us, and that function is not necessarily related to style (which is the other reason he admits older objects into his spaces, because they are, in his view, consummate examples of a living tradition). A modern house or apartment is about the space to live freely, unfettered, as one wishes. If Loos's *Raumplan*, seen from an outside vantage, might be regarded as constrictive, in Loos's view it is about the myriad ways that movement and perception can make us feel alive, fully integrated with the material world, and intensely aware of our surroundings.

All of the essays in this book are forays into these thoughts – into Loos's own rich and complex intellectual space. They are an effort to discern his message precisely and to comprehend its meanings. It is not a full exposition, but a series of probings – little journeys into a vital mind and a key moment in the history of architecture and design.

Austin, June 2018

1 | Becoming Loos

Part I | The Lessons of America

On July 2, 1893, Adolf Loos set off from Hamburg harbor aboard the steamship *Wieland* bound for New York. The ship, operated by the Hamburg-Amerikanische Packetfahrt Actien-Gesellschaft, one of many companies then plying the Atlantic transporting masses of immigrants to the United States, was old – its maiden voyage had taken place some twenty years before – and, at only 3,507 gross tons, small by the standards of the day. It was anything but a luxury liner. And Loos's accommodations could only be described as spartan. We know from the surviving ship manifest that he traveled as a *Kajüte* passenger, a class in steerage that offered lodging in a shared cabin deep in the ship's hold. The space was bare, cramped, and poorly ventilated, consisting of multiple, stacked berths on all four sides around a small central table.[1]

Loos's fellow suitemates, presumably all single young men like himself, were apt to have been poor immigrants, seeking a better life in the New World. Loos, by contrast, was a son of the middle class and, moreover, a university student; he was embarked not on a journey to a new life but what, from all appearances,

Adolf Loos, 1902. Bildarchiv, Österreichische Nationalbibliothek, Vienna.

SS *Wieland*, ca. 1893. Photo by J. S. Johnston for the Detroit Publishing Co. Library of Congress, Prints and Photographs Division, Washington, D. C.

he hoped would be a grand adventure. He had visions and dreams. But at that time, he could have hardly imagined what awaited him. The twelve-day passage, a good deal of which he must have spent pressed in the tiny compartment among strangers, was scarcely an auspicious start to what would turn out to be the transformative experience of his life and what in retrospect would be a key moment in the birth of modernism in architecture and design.

Loos's American sojourn has become the stuff of legend. Nearly every account of his life and work includes some discussion – shorter or longer – concerning what he allegedly saw and what he took away from the experience. The facts that have come down to us, however, are few and fleeting.

Loos himself provided much to his own mythology. His later writings are peppered with asides and remarks about his encounters with American life and culture – some of which don't bear up under careful scrutiny – and the supposed impact these had on him. Loos was not quite a serial fabulist, but he was certainly prone to embellishing his tales. This has made the task of working out what he actually saw and experienced all the more challenging.

The decided lack of reliable information has prompted a cottage industry of speculation on the part of latter-day scholars. A not insignificant amount of what has been written about Loos and America is, to be charitable, "creatively devised." (A better term would probably be "concocted.") Indeed, in spite of the recent outpouring of scholarly writing about Loos – some of it of very high quality – his American fable has not only persisted but has even swelled. It has become ever more challenging to separate fact from pure conjecture.

But a picture, once one begins to trim away what is factually flawed or merely supposition, does emerge, and it reveals a remarkable (if less full) tale. For, over the five years following his departure from Hamburg, the first three in America, the last two after his return to Europe, Loos would remake himself, and, in the process, come to formulate his own singular theories. How he arrived at his great insights is a story even more remarkable than the myths have it.

When Adolf Loos set off for New York that early July of 1893, he was twenty-two years old. One might best have described him at that moment as an ineffectual architecture student. He had had a pitiable educational experience in his early years, shunted off from one school to the next, flunking or just getting by, a record that he sustained at his last educational stop, the Königlich Sächsisches Technische Hochschule (Royal Saxon Polytechnic University) in Dresden. He spent just two years there, failing his exams at the end of his first year and leaving the school early the second.[2]

In his later starring role as a modernist idol, Loos would become inseparably bound up with the city of Vienna, with its urbanity and cultural refinement. But he was, in truth, very much a son of the provinces. Born in 1870 in the Moravian city of Brünn (Brno, Czech Republic) and raised there until he was sent off to boarding school, he had, by his own later admission, a rather insular childhood. One significant part of his evolution into a modernist prophet was his leave-taking from his provincial upbringing.[3] But his gradual transformation into the confident and polished man about town that he became by the early years of the new century would take some time.

Loos's father, also named Adolf Loos, was a master stonemason from Brno who had attended the Academy of Fine Arts in Vienna, the empire's elite finishing institution for artists, as a sculpture student. Afterward, in the early 1860s, the elder Loos returned home and established a workshop focused on making elaborate grave markers and stone detailing for buildings. From time to time, he fashioned artistic sculptures – mostly in the form of busts – for

| Loos house and workshop on Kounicova Street, Brno. Archiv města Brna.

members of the town's elite, in a style that combined nineteenth-century realism with a distilled classicism. Soon after his return, he married Marie Hertl, the daughter of a local government official. Young Adolf was the eldest of their three children.[4]

The house in which the family lived was connected via a small courtyard to the father's atelier. The young Loos spent hours in the shop observing the activities of his father and the journeymen and apprentices who worked for him. He reveled in the experience, in watching the men carefully cut and shape the stone, in observing how they selected the best pieces and how they avoided cracks and occlusions, in witnessing the sheer act of skilled craftspeople producing beautiful objects with their hands. He scrutinized and noted everything: how the stones were manipulated, how the designs were determined and transferred to the stones, how the men cut the blocks, how they wielded their hammers and chisels, how they polished and finished the surfaces.

Tragedy struck early, putting an abrupt end his childhood idyll. The death of his father, in 1879, when Loos was not quite nine, was a devastating blow for him. It was a loss that would stay with him for the remaining balance of his life.

Although we have no direct evidence of it, his profound attachment to craft and craftspeople was almost certainly bound up with his feelings for his father.

After his father's death, Loos's mother, with whom he had a strained relationship at best, sent him off to one boarding school after the next – to Brno and Iglau (Jihlava), in Moravia, and Melk, in Lower Austria. He did miserably in school. Energetic, perceptive, and, it seems, preternaturally sensitive to the world around him, he was not lacking in intelligence. But he had difficulties with his studies nearly from the outset, in part because he showed no interest at all in academic subjects (or, for that matter, even drawing: he received the lowest note in the course for freehand rendering at the Gymnasium in Melk), in part because at around age twelve he began to exhibit hearing problems that would leave him nearly completely deaf by the end of his life.[5]

The first significant alteration in the dismal course of his education came in 1885, when he enrolled in the Staatsgewerbeschule (State Trades School), in Reichenberg (Liberec, Czech Republic). He first studied machine building, but the following year he transferred to the architecture department. The next year, he transferred again, this time to the architecture department at the Staatsgewerbeschule in Brno. Among his classmates there were Josef Hoffmann and Hubert Gessner, both soon to launch important careers in Vienna. Loos, for once, did passably well: he completed the last of his coursework in the early summer of 1889, though it would take him nearly another year to achieve satisfactory scores on all of his examinations.[6]

That autumn he entered the Polytechnic University in Dresden. The school had a reputation as one of the best architecture faculties in Germany, and Loos, unusually, applied himself – at least a little – to his studies. Precisely what he took away from his time there is unclear. It was in this period that he was likely first exposed to the writings and ideas of Gottfried Semper, which would become a touchstone for his own theories. And he doubtless was able to polish and augment the hand and design skills he had acquired as a trade school student. Beyond that, he seems to have absorbed an awareness of the importance that the advent of new building technologies and materials was having for architecture, and a mounting unease with the language of late historicism – standard themes in the advanced architecture faculties of the day. Loos's dissatisfaction with the state of current practice was not an uncommon perspective then. Many younger German and Austrian architecture students in 1892 were restless, sensing the coming winds of change. Yet what was surely still indistinct for Loos was what direction that coming revolution might take, and what precisely it might consist of.

He spent the next year fulfilling his required military service in the Austrian army. During this time, he acquired a case of syphilis. He returned home to receive treatment. The episode only served to widen the distance between him and his mother. The therapy – which in that era consisted of repeated doses of mercury (Salvarsan, the first effective treatment against the disease, was not developed until 1910 by Nobel Prize winner Paul Ehrlich and his Japanese assistant Sahachiro Hata) – lessened the symptoms but left him infertile. While recovering, he applied, without success, to the Akademie der bildenden Künste (Academy of Fine Arts) in Vienna. With few other options open to him, he returned to the university in Dresden. He left again before the end of the summer term to take part in maneuvers with his army reserve unit. He then decided, quite suddenly, to travel to the United States to view the World's Columbian Exposition in Chicago.

The move was doubtless in some measure an attempt to escape his mother's control and find an exit from his desultory studies. In any event, it marked both an end to his relationship with her and to his formal education.[7] But Loos's reasons for his journey to the United States were also connected with at least two other aims. One, perhaps the principal one for Loos (even if he left it unstated), was to visit his father's brother, Friedrich (or Frederick, as he renamed himself) Loos, in Philadelphia.[8] The second was the prospect of seeing what was happening in America, to witness with his own eyes the rise of a new nation and a new culture.

Loos arrived in New York on July 14 and remained in the city for eight days.[9] About what he saw or how he reacted, he left no record – a pattern that was to continue throughout much of his time in America. He then journeyed to Philadelphia to visit his uncle Frederick and his family.[10]

Frederick Loos was a year older than Loos's father. Born in Vienna, he had completed training as a watchmaker before his departure for the United States, in 1850. Like many immigrants, he moved repeatedly, living for a time in and near Kansas City, Missouri, on what was then the frontier. Later, during the Civil War, he served as an officer in a Union regiment.[11] By the 1880s, he had settled in Pennsylvania, where he set up a shop at 726 Chestnut Street in downtown Philadelphia. He and his American-born wife, Mary, lived not far away with their eight children, including several around Loos's age.[12]

How long Loos initially remained with the family is uncertain. From the little we know about this period in his life, it was likely not more than a few weeks.[13] The stay served him in two crucial ways. It allowed him to begin to

017515. CHESTNUT STREET AND POST OFFICE, PHILADELPHIA, PA.
YE PARK

learn English (he had set off from Europe equipped only with twelve hours of instruction in English from the Berlitz school in Dresden).[14] He was also, it seems, able to reencounter through his uncle what he missed so greatly after his father's death: the relationship to a paternal figure.

During his time in Philadelphia, Loos visited another uncle, Benjamin, who had a farm in the nearby countryside.[15] "We traveled by train," he remembered, "then for an hour by foot. Along the way were many villas, winsome little houses with towers, gables, and verandas. These were farmhouses – America does not have country folk in the European sense. The 'farmer' is not like those in Europe. The women do not work in the fields."[16]

His commentary, written a decade afterward in his short-lived magazinelet, *Das Andere*, is characteristic of Loos's statements about his time in America. They are always in some portion perceptive: the newer farmhouses one found at the time did often resemble those of the burgeoning suburbs. But Loos's pronouncements also are in part invented or, at a minimum, a misreading. It was hardly the case that farmers in the United States were undifferentiated from urban dwellers. Still, Loos's observation that class distinctions were less sharply drawn than in Europe and that there was a shared sense of belonging – insights that did largely hold true – had for him enormous appeal. He thought this was a substantial attribute of what he began to call "abendländische Kultur" – Western culture. And the notion of a Western viewpoint – different from what he had known in his youth – became for him the antithesis of everything he loathed about the culture of Austria.

What, if anything else, Loos absorbed during his time with his uncle's family in Philadelphia is now impossible to say with any certainty. Burkhardt Rukschcio and Roland L. Schachel, in their massive biography of Loos, hint that Philadelphia's many neoclassical buildings must have in some way influenced his later ideas.[17] Likewise, Eduard Sekler, in an important article on Loos's American journey,

| Chestnut Street, Philadelphia, Pennsylvania, ca. 1900. Frederick Loos's shop was located in the 700 block. Library of Congress, Prints and Photographs Division, Washington, D. C.

| Benjamin Henry Latrobe, Frederick Graff et al., Fairmount Waterworks, Philadelphia, Pennsylvania. Historic American Engineering Record, Library of Congress, Prints and Photographs Division, Washington, D. C.

remarked on the possibility that the classical *Gesamtbild* (the collective urban landscape) of Philadelphia must have attracted Loos – without offering any evidence.[18] It is possible. But Loos could have witnessed related buildings almost everywhere he had traveled in Central Europe. Examples of neoclassical and Biedermeier architecture – even replica Greek temples – were nearly ubiquitous.

In the same vein, Sekler suggested that the building that housed Frederick Loos's shop on Chestnut Street, a typical commercial structure with a cast-iron façade and windows with rounded-over corners, showed "parallels with the rounded door corners" of Loos's design for the Ebenstein tailor salon, his first completed work after his return to Austria.[19] Such pronouncements – understandable when the evidence is otherwise so scarce – are, however, emblematic of the mythology that has grown up around Loos's time in America. The formula is always the same: Loos purportedly saw this or that building or object, and the influences or specific motifs show up in his later designs. So, Benedetto Gravagnuolo (who is otherwise quite good in his description of what Loos might have gleaned from his American soujourn), includes photographs of the Monadnock Building, a Chicago grain elevator, and other structures he purportedly encountered. Even more, though, he writes, "The similarity between the first interiors, designed or carried out by Loos and those of Richardson's houses (one thinks of the Sherman House, 1874–75 – from which Wright himself drew inspiration – or of the Cheney House, 1877) is so obvious as to be inescapable."[20]

But the effort to draw such connections – especially direct ones, as Sekler and Gravagnuolo do, is, at this remove, an exercise in mere speculation. It is possible, as Rukschcio and Schachel suggest, that Loos was in some way influenced by the works of Philadelphia's early classical architects, including Benjamin Latrobe and William Strickland. But the documentary support for such assertions is sketchy at best. Far more problematic, though, are statements like those of Sekler and Gravagnuolo. Did Loos see and draw directly from Richardson's architecture? Perhaps. Perhaps not. Or perhaps he only learned about Richardson later. Maybe Loos drew from the Chestnut store façade for the Ebenstein commission. Perhaps, but perhaps not.[21]

Loos's time in Chicago has been the most fertile subject for speculation about what he supposedly took from America. There are many suggestions in the Loos literature that his time there was the crucial point for him, and that his later architecture owed much to what he saw there. It turns out, however, on a closer look, that Loos's stay in Chicago was brief – only for a single week.[22]

Fairgrounds, World's Columbian Exposition, Chicago, 1893. Photograph by Frances Benjamin Johnston. Library of Congress, Prints and Photographs Division, Washington, D. C.

That his visit was so abbreviated – something that is often left out of accounts of his American period – almost certainly had to do with the fact that he had little money and needed to be frugal. It was unquestionably a crucial week for him. From his later statements, we can safely assume that he did indeed visit the World's Columbian Exposition – his expressed goal at the outset of his American adventure – and that the encounter would come to have a shattering effect on him. In one of the essays he penned for the *Neue Freie Presse* in Vienna after his return to Europe, he recorded some of his impressions.

> If one remains bound to the soil of his homeland, he is never truly aware of what treasures his own country holds; what is excellent is accepted as a matter of course. But once one has seen something of the world, one's assessment of the indigenous changes. Gods are overthrown, pygmies raised aloft.
>
> When, some years ago, I left the homeland in order to get to know architecture and handicraft on the other side of the Atlantic, I was still fully convinced of the superiority of German

> craftsmen. It was with a feeling of great pride that I made my way through the German and Austrian sections in Chicago. I looked down on the stirrings of American "applied arts" with a pitying smile. How my feelings have altered! The experience of my years over there means that I still blush to think what a disgrace the exhibition of the German craft industry in Chicago was. All those magnificent masterworks, those stylish showpieces! Nothing but vulgar fakery.[23]

It is doubtful, though, that while making the rounds at the exposition Loos's "Gods were overthrown" suddenly or entirely. If one reads the passage carefully, it is clear that it took him some time to digest what he had seen and to begin to make sense of it. He implies as much in his own description. He writes: "How my feelings have altered!" – not that they *were* changed at that moment.

Yet we can probably assume that what he said in the main about the experience is correct: the exhibition had a powerful impact on him. Precisely what he observed and how he initially reacted is now lost to us, though it was unquestionably unsettling for him. From all indications, it was only a beginning, the start of a process of rethinking the proper course for design and what that might mean. What he experienced at the Chicago exposition was, from all appearances, only a provocation, a first shaking of his previously held beliefs. The course of his reevaluation would go on for some time.

What else Loos might have seen in Chicago is also now only a matter for conjecture. Like Gravagnuolo, other scholars have suggested – again, without firm evidence – that he was affected by what he glimpsed of the architecture of the Chicago School, and that he would come to recycle his impressions in some fashion in his work.[24] Much ink has been dispensed about his supposed reactions to the works of H. H. Richardson, Louis Sullivan, or, even, Frank Lloyd Wright (who, in 1893, was just beginning his career and would hardly have drawn Loos's notice). Hermann Czech and Wolfgang Mistelbauer, for example, have pointed to the similarities between the combination of the bay window and pillar in the Rookery and the Studebaker Building and Loos's handling of such arrangements.[25]

But just how much time Loos would have had to inspect the new architecture of the city is an open question. If it is correct that he spent only a single week in the city, then it could not have been much. We can probably safely presume that he was at the fairgrounds for at least several days during his stay – if not more. The scale of the exhibition was mammoth: the exhibition grounds

Display of German porcelain wares at the World's Columbian Exposition, Chicago, 1893. Private collection.

Display of German fountains at the World's Columbian Exposition, Chicago, 1893. Private collection.

Louis Sullivan, Transportation Building at the World's Columbian Exposition, Chicago, 1893. Private collection.

Louis Sullivan, Wainwright Building, St. Louis, 1891. Private collection.

extended over six hundred acres, and the fair's fourteen halls and other free-standing pavilions housed sixty-five thousand exhibits. Even if he saw only a portion of the displays, he would not have had much time to see the rest of the city. Loos, from all that we know, was acutely sensitive; it is possible that he hastily absorbed a great deal. But Chicago was already a big city; there was much for a young foreigner to take in.

There have been repeated suggestions on the part of some scholars that possible clues to his encounters can be found in what he collected. Surviving in the Loos archive are various postcards and photographs of sites or buildings he supposedly visited throughout his time in America. That Loos took the trouble to assemble such images is evidence, they argue, that the works in question held some special significance for him. The historian Ludwig Münz, for instance, made much of a postcard of the Bunker Hill Monument in Boston that he found in Loos's papers. Münz thought the disconnectedness of the tower and an adjacent temple-front neoclassical building was quintessentially "American," and that the same odd pairing was repeated in several of Loos's subsequent projects.[26]

But it is uncertain whether Loos even collected many of these images during his time in America. As Sekler has noted, two of the photographs of buildings Loos possessed, of the Bowling Green Offices and the W. & G. Audsley Company, both in New York, bear the stamp of the S. Bloch publishing house in Vienna.[27] Also among Loos's papers are images of the Flatiron Building and the hotels Vanderbilt and Belmont – all constructed after Loos's time in the city. And there are two postcards of the Railway Exchange Building on South Michigan Avenue in Chicago.[28] The seventeen-story steel-framed building was the work of Frederick P. Dinkelberg of the D. H. Burnham Company. It is a consummate example of the Chicago School from the time. That Loos owned two copies does hint that he had some special interest in the work. But the building was completed in 1904; Loos could not have seen it during his time there, and how he came to own the postcards is unknown.

Equally uncertain is how much he actually saw of H. H. Richardson's or Louis Sullivan's works, or, indeed, those of any of the other progressive Chicago architects. It is likely that he inspected Sullivan's Transportation Building on the exposition fairgrounds since it was quite large and on a prominent site. But if he did, he failed to comment on it. Beyond that, we have few, if any, clues. Either on his trip to or from Chicago, Loos may have stopped in St. Louis, and he may have seen Sullivan's recently completed Wainwright Building. It is a tantalizing idea to think of him contemplating one of Sullivan's masterworks – and all that he might have gleaned from inspecting it. The most we probably can say with any semblance of truth, though, is that he witnessed the power and novelty of Chicago (and also perhaps, St. Louis) commercial architecture from the 1880s and early 1890s, and that it must have provided him a patent contrast with what he knew from Central Europe.

After his brief stay in Chicago, Loos returned to Philadelphia. He later put the timing of his return at "about six weeks after his first arrival," indicating that it must have been in late August or early September.[29] Soon afterward, one of his cousins died of typhoid. Loos later told how he met his aunt, the wife of his uncle Benjamin, on a train on the way to the funeral, but that he did not recognize her at first. She was elegantly dressed, in a manner that belied the fact that she was a farmer's wife, and very different from the way he had previously seen her. It was another instance, as Loos would come to write, of how the distinctions between social classes had been eroded in America – and another emblem, he thought, of "Western culture."[30]

Sometime after the funeral, his uncle Frederick moved the family to a house out in one of the Philadelphia suburbs. Loos, who had hoped to work together with the deceased cousin (who had been a builder), now had to look for other options.[31] The "Panic of 1893," which led to a serious economic downturn in the United States, made finding employment, especially for a marginally skilled foreigner whose grasp of English was shaky at best, exceedingly difficult. To save money, Loos repeatedly walked into the city from his uncle's house – a considerable distance – to search for work. But he could secure only a few menial and temporary jobs. He would say afterward that these were the worst months of his life, and that the Christmas he spent with his uncle's family was "the saddest" he "ever experienced."[32] Whether he had some sort of falling out with his uncle and aunt, he never revealed. (Given Loos's temperament, it is entirely possible that he quarreled with them.) In any event, a short time afterward, about four months after his return to Philadelphia, Loos left and went to New York. It would become a turning point for him.

Loos spent more than two years in the city. New York – not Chicago or Philadelphia – became the main laboratory of his learning, the place where he began to form fully his own personal and distinctive ideas about design. Up to this time, to judge from the little that we know, it appears that Loos was still mostly observing the world around him, often passively and without endeavoring to put together a clear theoretical framework. But slowly, gradually, he started to process what he witnessed and to formulate his ideas. The experiences he had during

View of the Bunker Hill Monument designed by Solomon Willard, Boston, 1825–43. Library of Congress, Prints and Photographs Division, Washington, D. C.

Frederick P. Dinkelberg, D. H. Burnham Company. Railway Exchange Building, Chicago, 1903–04. Library of Congress, Prints and Photographs Division, Washington, D. C.

New York City, ca. 1894. View up Broadway with Post Office building on the right. Photo by J. S. Johnston. Library of Congress, Prints and Photographs Division, Washington, D. C.

New York City, ca. 1894. View toward Shoe and Leather Bank. Photo by J. S. Johnston. Library of Congress, Prints and Photographs Division, Washington, D. C.

his time in New York – and, even more, his impressions of the city and everything in it – began to join together in his thoughts. What he sensed, what he came to discern, if only hazily at first, was a radical alternative to nearly everything he had been taught or believed up to then. The years he spent there were his true *Lehrjahre*; they were a first important step in his mature formation.

Richard Neutra, who attended Loos's private architecture school in Vienna in the period just before the outbreak of World War I, recorded in his memoir *Life and Shape* what Loos had told him about his years in New York.

> He landed in New York and went through a rather horrible time in the slums of lower Manhattan. He had no money, and he never succeeded even in getting a job as a draftsman. Instead, he did all kinds of chores, from night-shift dishwasher to auxiliary day dishwasher. When he, with his serene trace of a grin and the low voice of a deaf man, which he was all his life, told of his endless job hunts and of finally making a living, he took advantage of the fact that in German the expression is not "dishwasher" but "vessel-washer" – *Nachtgeschirrwäscher* – which sounded to German listeners like a washer of pots de chambre, a rather disheartening job for a pioneer architect.[33]

When Loos arrived in New York, he found a room at the Young Men's Christian Association (YMCA). It was the first extended period that he was entirely on his own in America. The weeks he spent there, however, hardly represented a direct immersion into American life: most of those living in the building were recent immigrants, many of them Germans, Austrians, and Jews.[34] That pattern would repeat for him throughout his stay in the city. After leaving the YMCA, Loos, as he told Neutra, found a temporary job and lodging in Lower Manhattan.

> [I] was helping in a little barbershop on Fourteenth Street – which shop, by the way, had a very interesting entrance of glass beads, such as I later used at my Goldman and Salatsch tailoring store on Michaelerplatz. One of the barbers brought me to a cousin of his, a Jewish tailor who lived in the basement of a brownstone house two blocks east of the Bowery. The tailor worked, needled, cut, and fitted in his basement; but he had a little rear room where he hung the suits. He rented it to me, since

> there was a short couch to sleep on. Thus I lived with the Jewish tailor and his family, who were very nice people. I stayed for many months, but I could not find a steady job. I tried everything, while the tailor and his wife kindheartedly waited for me to pay the rent. He even loaned me some cash, and I advertised in the paper that I was an expert on heraldry and could design a coat of arms for any new-rich family in New York. Well, I got an order here and there, but I could not make a living, and occasionally had to go back to my odd jobs of the "night pot-washing" variety.[35]

Loos's time spent performing odd jobs was not entirely without recompense. He wrote years afterward that during this period he found employment working for a company that produced marquetry. He stated that he performed various tasks: transferring the drawings, shading the wood by burning it with hot sand, inserting the finishing veneers, and cutting parquet. The time he spent working there, he asserted, gave him a new appreciation of making things with his hands, which was "more important than the fact that I studied at the polytechnic."[36]

But the job, like all he found in his first year in New York, proved short-term. According to his own telling, he often went days – possibly even weeks – without income. When he was not working, he recalled that he sometimes stood in line at various department stores to receive free bread or at a company that gave away coffee and sugar.[37] Much later, he claimed that he worked for a brief time as a music and theater critic for a German-language newspaper and that he spent time as an opera extra. He wrote a wonderful send-up of his purported participation in a performance by the famed Australian soprano Nellie Melba.[38] It is more than curious, though, that no direct evidence of his efforts as a critic has yet come to light – no published reviews under his name, no other documentary evidence, nothing aside from Loos's own account.[39] Perhaps it was his effort to put the best face on what for him was an exceedingly painful time, living hand to mouth in the city, without much to show for it.

Loos would write subsequently that sometime afterward, toward the end of 1894, or about a year after he had arrived back in New York, he found (contrary to Neutra's statement) a position as a draftsman in the office of an architect.[40] Again, the name of the architect in question has not come down to us, nor do we have any record of what Loos did over that period. It was almost certainly not a well-known or respected architect; otherwise, Loos would have mentioned his name later on. But Loos may well have learned a good deal about the actual practice of architecture. The only thing that is certain is that he must have found better and more steady work, because he was evidently able to save enough money to pay for his passage back to Europe and to provide stopovers in London and Paris along the way. (He had departed Europe with a one-way ticket.)[41]

From what he tells us, Loos's day-to-day life, despite this period of outward stability, remained a struggle. His situation was precarious – at least, until his final year – and he lived and sometimes worked among poor recent immigrants And yet, he reveled in it all, and he came away, as Neutra describes, with a remarkably – almost improbably – positive view of America.

> Loos had the most negative experience a gifted, aspiring immigrant can have, worse than any Slovak miner who ends up working in a Pennsylvania coal seam. He was a trained person and one of genius. I don't know how good his schooling was, but he was a most intelligent, human young man. In the United States he did nothing but menial work. He could never make both ends meet. But he loved the country. It was an unhappy, unforgettable love. Yet he had the most interesting stories to tell, and in spite of all external failures, he came back to the old country and Vienna, not broke, but with an enriched heart and with the most glowing enthusiasm for the country of his choice. I have never met any person, either in this or any other land, who was as enthusiastic about the "States" as Adolf Loos.[42]

What Loos seemingly most valued, what formed his attachment to America most enduringly and would become the substance of his later philosophy, as Neutra recorded, was the directness and practicality of American life.

> Loos continued to admire and love Americans, kitchen chefs, hotel managers, barbers, efficient bank tellers, El conductors, pushcart peddlers, and shoeshine boys ... His Americans were extremely fine human material, particularly through forgetting about the so-called sophisticated education and culture and those things that were exaggeratedly valued in European countries, especially in that cultural capital of Europe, which was then Vienna.[43]

This is the picture that has been passed down to us: Loos as the fervent admirer of American mores and practicality. It is doubtless correct in the main. Loos did come to value deeply a new "essentialism." His living on the margins helped to open his eyes because it forced him out of his previous bourgeois complacency. But something else evidently began to form in his mind. By the time he departed America, he had a profound alteration of his convictions.

The key moment may well have stemmed from an experience he described to the writer and critic Robert Scheu after he had settled in Vienna. It is worth quoting at length from what Scheu wrote about the episode because it portrays in detail what might have been the path of his intellectual advance.

> The epiphany came in America. [Loos] related that he was still filled with misunderstandings about what constitutes beauty, prejudices that he had absorbed in the architecture schools, as he was walking around the exhibitions of applied arts, and had sought there certain forms of embellishment. It is a fledgling land, though, where iron technology is utilized so resolutely and uninhibitedly; a country where the trees are felled in a primeval forest and laid crossways beneath the railroad tracks. Through human toil, the steel bands come to span chasms and waterfalls, and telegraph wires are extended across the prairies. And it is beautiful. A coruscating beauty, a singular conjunction of economics and technology with green, wild nature – in a word, style. To render it into a set of aesthetic principles – that is the real task. Admittedly this style is present only in a raw state; its conceptualization and reduction into a single idea must first be undertaken in a human mind. We can gather that Adolf Loos performed just such an act, and we can rank this achievement even higher than anything visible and tangible he has produced. Over there, he conjured up the image of a style that the country itself had only possessed for a short time.
>
> It was in New York, where a suitcase in a store attracted his attention. A leather case, wrapped with copper banding. The next morning, he had a realization: the suitcase he had seen the day before – that was the modern style! From that moment on, he began to break with it all; everything that was false, wrong, or misconceived, he decried. His motto became: That which is practical

Advertisement for a suitcase manufactured by the Abel and Bach Company, Milwaukee, Wisconsin, ca. 1900, with an image of a design likely similar to the one Loos admired in his time in New York. Private collection.

> is beautiful! This elementary idea exploded all his received beliefs [and] opened his eyes to the secret lands of Great Britain and Greece. The Greeks work only with practical aims, without considering in the least the concept of beauty. ... Are there still those who work like the Greeks today? Oh yes, it is the English and the engineers as a profession.[44]

When Scheu wrote this, in 1909, Loos had already undertaken the necessary steps to build his keen insights into a comprehensive design philosophy. But the process of casting the main outlines of his philosophy, it seems from everything we know, would take Loos another several years after he left America.

There were two central elements of his new understanding. The first was that modernism was inherently practical. Bound up with this was Loos's belief that that which is practical is simple, and, by extension, that which is practical is also intrinsically beautiful. Modernism thus implied a direct and pure expression of an object's function. This would all become dogma among progressive architects and designers some quarter of a century hence. His second idea, however, was perhaps even more profound: modernism did not need to be invented; it already existed. It could be found wherever and whenever craftspeople or ordinary manufacturers made an honest effort to solve an everyday problem. And it was in objects of daily use – like the suitcase Loos had seen in the window – that the manifestation of modern reality could be most readily discerned. Fleshing out the full consequences of these two ideas and how they could be adapted to a practicable design strategy were for him the next significant step.

The intellectual force of Loos's sudden breakthrough has occasioned some to question whether he might have been influenced by something else, something he may have encountered or perhaps read. Sekler, writing in the mid 1980s, suggested that Loos might have been familiar with the essays of the American sculptor Horatio Greenough, who very early, in the 1840s and 1850s, put forward the notion of a radical functionality as an aesthetic concept, or the writings of Louis Sullivan, who similarly articulated his ideas about the relationship between the practical and the formal.[45] Did Loos read Greenough or Sullivan at this time? Or did he simply arrive at his idea about functionality on his own? We have no clarion indication either way. But Loos's own explanation of how he had come to his startling realization does ring true. His quiet observation of American pragmatism, his penchant for craft, and his admiration for objects well and simply made, were, from all we know, the determining factors – not anything he took up and read at the time.

That it was also objects – or better, the lessons stemming from objects he had come in contact with – rather than works of architecture, that apparently drew the greater share of Loos's attention contradicts much of what later commentators have written. It is striking that after his return to Austria Loos wrote or said very little about the American buildings he had seen. (Schachel has contended – correctly in my view – that if American architecture had really been so important to Loos, "he would have returned to America to keep up on the current trends," which he never did.[46]) The references he makes in his writings and what those who listened to his tales later recorded were focused very largely on articles of daily use – invariably the products of handicraft. And where his discussion is not fixated on objects (and their lessons), it mostly has to do with the practicality of American culture. Loos may well have drawn from time to time on the buildings he had seen in America in his own architecture (though it would be difficult, if not impossible, to prove definitively which buildings influenced him or how). But for his intellectual formation, architecture seems to have assumed less of a role.

What speaks also for the verity of Loos's assertions about his epiphany arising from seeing the suitcase in New York is that in 1896, when his breakthrough presumably came, he still had much cerebral work to do. His formation as a theorist was then still ongoing. Schachel, again, very perceptively, has suggested that Loos's whole American experience was less about what he saw or what inspired him than the role it played on his personal development. And the "stimulation" of his American experiences in the aggregate, he writes, "naturally had a more lasting impact on his entire body of work" than any particular forms or motifs or whole buildings he might have inspected.[47]

In the spring of that year – not quite fully his third in America – Loos returned to Europe. His ostensible reason was to take part in his army reserve unit's summer maneuvers; had he not reported it would have been regarded as desertion.[48] It would have been difficult for him to return after that time. But he was then already resolved, it appears, to go back to Austria – and to restart his career there.

Part II | The Strategy of Sorting

Significantly for Loos's intellectual advance, he made a prolonged layover in London on his return voyage. About what he saw, or even how long he was there, we again have almost no information. And concerning what he made of it all we also have scant evidence, other than the scattered remarks he would come to make in his later writings about English sensibilities and practices. We can guess, though, at some of what he might have seen. Given his many comments about English tailoring, shoes, and hats, he must have spent a great deal of his time in shops (perhaps on Savile Row or Bond Street), or strolling along the streets and peering in store windows. (He evidently purchased a new wardrobe while he was in the city, which must have also contributed to his lifelong admiration for English tailoring.) He must have also meticulously observed the people he encountered, noting how they dressed and how they interacted. Since almost all of his subsequent commentaries involved articles of daily use (usually English clothing) or cultural mores, we can probably safely presume that he was again attracted more to these things than to architecture. Whatever the case, his stay

Peter Altenberg, ca. 1900.
From Peter Altenberg,
Was der Tag mir zuträgt
(Berlin, 1901), frontispiece.

Karl Kraus, ca. 1895.
Private collection.

– and a follow-on, apparently shorter stop in Paris – confirmed for him his belief in the superiority of "Western" culture and its potential as a model for Austria. It further served to bolster his faith in the centrality of craft to modernism and his conviction that the new style had already made its appearance.

After fulfilling his army obligations that summer, Loos moved to Vienna. He worked for some months for the architect Carl Mayreder. An adjunct professor at the Vienna Technische Hochscule (Technical University), Mayreder was a man of progressive views (his wife Rosa Mayreder was a leader of the feminist movement) and a competent and thoughtful practitioner. But Loos detested the work he did – which in stylistic terms was more or less in keeping with the language of late historicism – and he soon left Mayreder's employ.

It was in this period that Loos met the writers Peter Altenberg and Karl Kraus. The men – both fixtures of the city's literary demimonde – offered Loos a crash course in the latest views and discussions in a comprehensive array of areas, from letters and history to science and psychology. Kraus, in particular, who was well read and acutely intellectual (in a way that Loos was not), appears to have taken the lead in acquainting him with the main currents of the day. What Loos learned would become an integral part of the substance of his mature theories.

Altenberg and Kraus became Loos's constant companions. They met regularly in the evenings, spending hours together, often late into the night. Loos also knew (or came to know) many of the young architects in the city. But he held his distance, only rarely socializing or spending time with them. (Schachel writes of his "self-chosen splendid isolation."[49]) Altenberg and Kraus – and a few other writers from their circle, in particular Otto Stoessl and Robert Scheu – formed the principal cohort of his first years in the capital.

Loos's ability to formulate what was an impressively original set of theoretical assumptions about the new design probably had much to do with the fact that he remained outside the architectural mainstream. At the very moment when the Vienna Secession was being formed, and the specific Austrian variant of the Jugendstil was being fashioned, Loos was conceiving a set of doctrines that stood apart from, and, indeed, in opposition to, the Secessionists and all that they held dear.

It was in this period that he came to the work that would define the next several years of his life: writing for various newspapers and cultural journals. His first effort, penned for *Die Zeit*, a weekly cultural review put out by the writer and dramatist Hermann Bahr, set the tone for his future essays: it is highly opinionated and even more highly critical. In spite of its rather generic title, "The Student Exhibition of the School of Arts and Crafts," the piece is a methodical and penetrating assault on the school (the Vienna Kunstgewerbeschule) and its curriculum. Loos asserts that the institution's overly academic approach and its emphasis on "art," rather than making and problem-solving, was ruining the crafts: "Away with all this senseless drawing, away with paper art! What we should be doing now is reexamining life, our habits, our need for comfort and practicality to discover new forms, new lines! Off you go, young students, art is an obstacle to be surmounted and left behind."[50]

Loos's condemnation of art education in the crafts would become for him an unwavering theme. Fundamental to his argument is the effort to establish an all-encompassing distinction between art and craft. The purpose of art, Loos believed, is to make works to be contemplated and to express meaning; the purpose of craft, on the other hand, is to make objects that address a need, that fulfill an everyday necessity. And the problem he saw with most of Viennese design was that these two very different tasks were being conflated. The English, unlike the Austrians, he insists, understood this.

> Over the past ten years the whole world has been marching forward under England's leadership ... and it is high time we catch up before it is too late. ... How life has changed abroad! Painters, sculptors, architects are leaving their comfortable studios behind them, saying farewell to high art, and turning to the anvil, the loom, the potter's wheel, and the carpenter's bench.[51]

Here Loos is referencing the British Arts and Crafts movement and its emphasis on addressing the circumstances of everyday design. The issue for him, though, not only involved the return to craft, but a penchant for "ordinariness," for solving commonplace problems. In another of his early essays for *Die Zeit*, a review of the 1897 Christmas exhibition at the Österreichisches Museum für Kunst und Industrie (Austrian Museum of Art and Industry), which adjoined the School of Arts and Crafts, he applauds the museum's new director, Arthur von Scala, for showing not the designs intended for the wealthy and the nobility (which continued to be used as models for so much of what was being produced for the marketplace), but those of, and for, the middle class.

> Why are historical objects from middle-class households so little known? Because comparatively few have come down to us. The bourgeois wear their furniture out; they utilize it daily, and when it has reached the end of its useful life they chop it up for firewood. ... Very different is princely furniture. It was never or seldom actually put to use and proclaimed its aristocratic and unsullied character by being richly decorated with motifs from classical architecture. ... Its purpose was to represent ostentation, to bear witness to wealth, splendor, taste, and the love of art of its owner. ... And now the present century has misused these museum pieces by taking them as models for practical items.[52]

Loos's intention in this essay, in part, is a full-frontal assault on historicism, on the falsity of using a Louis XIV desk or a bed modeled on Napoleon's for the ordinary bourgeois interior. But he is after something far more consequential: the idea that an essential feature of modern life is authenticity, and that "aping the aristocracy" was passing out of fashion. What the new age demanded, Loos asserts, is to abhor any form of fakery or tasteless imitation.

What stands out in these first essays is not only the brilliance of what Loos is expressing, but the supreme confidence with which he affirms it. By the end of 1897, he had found his voice; he would never again remain quietly on the sidelines. Even more arresting is the quality of his prose. It is pellucid, evocative, and forceful in a way that is wholly unlike any other architectural writer of his day. Absent are the florid excesses of the fin de siècle: the overheated metaphors, the overlong sentences, the intertwining phrases. Loos's German is pure, direct, unalloyed – in a word: modern. How much he had Altenberg and Kraus (who were both refined stylists in their own right) to thank for that is not possible now to determine. But Loos, even in these initial attempts, already exhibited the signs of becoming a superlative writer.

Over the course of the early months of 1898, Loos wrote several additional reviews for *Die Zeit* and another related publication, *Die Wage*.[53] It was an entirely different commission, however, that would offer him the opportunity to develop his ideas into a full-blown theoretical construct. By the time he finished these essays, he had elaborated the core elements of his philosophy and all he would build on – intellectually and in his design work – over the next three and a half decades.

The task put before Loos in the spring of that year was to produce a series of reviews of the Jubilee exhibition marking the fiftieth anniversary of Emperor Franz Joseph's ascension to the throne for Austria's leading newspaper, the Vienna *Neue Freie Presse*. It was a plum job. Precisely how Loos came to it remains a mystery. Possibly his first few essays had attracted attention. It is more likely, though, that someone among his acquaintances had a connection and recommended him. The twenty articles he would write over the six months the exhibition ran would make his name for the first time, and, more significantly, allow him to think his way through nearly every problem of contemporary design.

The exhibition opened on May 7, 1898. It was held in a group of mostly temporary buildings in the Prater, Vienna's great public park. Loos's first review, an overall assessment of the fairgrounds and its buildings, appeared the following day. It begins with an extraordinary statement about the situation of architecture and design, one Loos must have known very well would arouse consternation.

> It happened overnight. For a whole century, our architects have been struggling with an unruly age; for a whole century, we have been searching for an original building style that would put its stamp on our time. One was constantly forced to turn to existing

| Rotunda at the Kaiser Jubiläumsausstellung (Imperial Jubilee exhibition), Vienna, 1898. Bildarchiv, Österreichische Nationalbibliothek, Vienna.

| Adolf Loos, "Die Intérieurs in der Rotunda," *Neue Freie Presse*, July 12, 1898, p. 16. ANNO – Historische Zeitungen und Zeitschriften, Österreichische Nationalbibliothek, Vienna.

> styles, which then would be slightly modified for our culture. The call for a new style grew ever more shrill, ever more urgent, and yet the style itself seemed ever more distant. And now, suddenly, it is here and trying to gain entry into Vienna, for it is still *ante portas.*[54]

In a few spare and forthright sentences, Loos managed to portray the situation then confronting architects and designers: the overriding crisis of nineteenth-century aesthetic culture brought on by the failure to find a fitting expression, and the problem of discovering a suitable means to articulate the substance of the new industrial epoch. Most poignantly, though, he writes about the advent of the new style.

Wiener Jubiläums-Ausstellung.

Die Intérieurs in der Rotunde.

In meinem letzten Berichte habe ich recht ketzerische Forderungen aufgestellt. Weder der Archäologe, noch der Decorateur, noch der Architekt, noch der Maler oder der Bildhauer soll uns die Wohnung einrichten. Ja, wer soll es denn dann thun? Nun ganz einfach: Jeder sei sein eigener Decorateur.

Allerdings werden wir dann in keinen „stylvollen" Wohnungen wohnen können. Aber dieser „Styl", der Styl mit den Gänsefüßchen, ist auch gar nicht nöthig. Was ist denn dieser Styl überhaupt? Er läßt sich schwer definiren. Meiner Meinung nach fand jene wackere Hausfrau auf die Frage, was stylvoll sei, die beste Antwort: Wenn auf dem „Nachtkastel" ein Löwenkopf ist, und dieser Löwenkopf ist dann auf dem Sofa, auf dem Schrank, auf den Betten, auf den Sesseln, auf dem Waschtisch, kurz auf allen Gegenständen des Zimmers gleichfalls angebracht, so heißt dieses Zimmer stylvoll. Hand aufs Herz, meine Herren Gewerbetreibenden, haben Sie nicht redlich dazu beigetragen, eine solche widersinnige Meinung ins Volk zu bringen? Nicht immer war es ein Löwenkopf. Aber eine Säule, ein Knopf, eine Balustrade wurde immer in alle Möbel hineingepreßt, bald verlängert, bald verkürzt, bald verdickt, bald verdünnt.

Solche Zimmer tyrannisirten ihren armen Besitzer. Wehe dem Unglücklichen, wenn er es gewagt hätte, sich selbst etwas hinzuzukaufen! Denn diese Möbel vertrugen absolut kein anderes in ihrer Nähe. Bekam man etwas geschenkt, konnte man es nirgends hinstellen. Und wenn man die Wohnung wechselte und im neuen Heim nicht genau dieselben Zimmergrößen vorfand, dann war es auf immer mit der „stylvollen" Wohnung vorbei. Dann mußte vielleicht gar der altdeutsche Decorations-Divan in den blauen Rococosalon gestellt werden und der barocke Schrank in das Empire-Sitzzimmer. Schrecklich!

Wie gut hatte es doch dagegen der dumme Bauer oder der arme Arbeiter oder die alte Jungfer. Die hatten solche Sorgen nicht. Die waren nicht stylvoll eingerichtet. Eines kam von da her, das Andere von dort. Alles durcheinander. Doch was ist das? Die Maler, denen man doch so viel Geschmack zugetraut hatte, ließen unsere prächtigen Wohnungen links liegen und malten immer Intérieurs der dummen Bauern, der armen Arbeiter und der alten Jungfern. Wie man nur so etwas für schön finden kann? Denn schön ist, so wurde gelehrt, nur die stylvolle Wohnung.

Aber die Maler hatten Recht. Sie, die für alle Aeußerlichkeiten des Lebens, Dank ihrer geübten und trainirten Augen, einen viel schärferen Blick haben als andere Menschen, haben das Hohle, das Aufgeblasene, das Fremde, das Unharmonische unserer stylvollen Wohnungen stets erkannt. Die Menschen passen nicht zu diesen Räumen und die Räume nicht zu diesen Menschen. Wie sollten sie denn auch? Der Architekt, der Decorateur kennt seinen Auftraggeber kaum dem Namen nach. Und wenn der Bewohner diese Räume hundertmal käuflich erworben hat, es sind doch nicht *seine* Zimmer. Sie bleiben immer das geistige Eigenthum desjenigen, der sie erdacht hat. Auf den Maler konnten sie daher nicht wirken, es fehlte ihnen jeder geistige Zusammenhang mit dem Bewohner, es fehlte ihnen jenes Etwas, das sie eben im Zimmer des dummen Bauers, des armen Arbeiters, der alten Jungfer fanden: die Intimität.

Ich bin Gott sei Dank noch in keiner stylvollen Wohnung aufgewachsen. Damals kannte man das noch nicht. Jetzt ist es leider auch in meiner Familie anders geworden. Aber damals! Hier der Tisch, ein ganz verrücktes krauses Möbel, ein Ausziehtisch mit einer fürchterlichen Schlosserarbeit. Aber *unser* Tisch, *unser* Tisch! Wißt ihr, was das heist? Wißt ihr welche herrlichen Stunden wir da verlebt haben? Wenn die Lampe brannte! Wie ich als kleiner Bub' mich Abends nie von ihm trennen konnte, und Vater immer das Nachtwächterhorn imitirte, so daß ich ganz erschreckt ins Kinderzimmer lief! Und hier der Schreibtisch! Und hier der Tintenfleck darauf. Schwester Hermine hat hier als ganz kleines Baby die Tinte vergossen. Und hier die Bilder der Eltern! Welch schreckliche Rahmen! Aber es war das Hochzeitsgeschenk der Arbeiter des Vaters. Und hier der altmodische Sessel! Ein Ueberbleibsel aus dem Hausstande der Großmutter. Und hier ein gestickter Pantoffel, in dem man die Uhr aufhängen kann; Schwester Irma's Kindergartenarbeit. Jedes Möbel, jedes Ding, jeder Gegenstand erzählt eine Geschichte, die Geschichte der Familie. Die Wohnung war nie fertig; sie entwickelte sich mit uns und wir in ihr. Wol war kein Styl darin. Das heißt kein fremder, kein alter. Aber einen Styl hatte die Wohnung, den Styl ihrer Bewohner, den Styl der Familie.

Als die Zeit immer gebieterischer die Forderung nach der stylvollen Wohnung erhob — alle Bekannten waren schon altdeutsch eingerichtet, und da kann man doch nicht zurückbleiben — da wurde der ganze alte Plunder herausgeworfen. Plunder für jeden Anderen, für die Familie ein Heiligthum. Der Rest ist — Tapezierer.

Nun haben wir es aber satt bekommen. Wir wollen wieder in unseren eigenen vier Wänden Herren sein. Sind wir geschmacklos, gut, so werden wir uns geschmacklos einrichten. Haben wir Geschmack, um so besser. Von unserem Zimmer wollen wir uns aber nicht mehr tyrannisiren lassen. Wir kaufen Alles zusammen, Alles, wie wir es eben nach und nach brauchen können, wie es uns gefällt.

Wie es uns gefällt! Ja, da hätten wir ja doch den Styl, nach dem wir so lange gefahndet, den wir immer in die Wohnung herein haben wollten. Ein Styl, der nicht von den gleichen Löwenköpfen, sondern von dem Geschmacke oder wegenmeiner Ungeschmacke eines Menschen, einer Familie abhängig war und sich danach gestaltete. Das gleiche, gemeinsame Band, das alle Möbel im Raume mit einander verbindet, bestände eben darin, daß sein Besitzer die Auswahl getroffen hat. Und selbst wenn derselbe, insbesondere was die Farbenauswahl anbelangt, etwas sprunghaft vorgehen sollte, es gebe noch immer kein Unglück. So eine mit der Familie gewordene Wohnung verträgt schon etwas. Wenn man nämlich in ein „stylvolles" Zimmer auch nur Ein Nippesstückchen hineinstellt, das nicht dazu gehört, so kann das ganze Zimmer verdorben werden. Im Familienzimmer geht es sofort in dem Raume vollständig auf. Ist doch so ein Zimmer wie eine Violine. Die kann man einspielen, jenes einwohnen.

Unberührt von diesen Ausführungen bleiben selbstverständlich jene Räume, die nicht zum Wohnen benützt werden. Bad und die Toilette werde ich vom Installateur, die Küche vom betreffenden Fachmanne einrichten lassen. Und vollends solche Räume, die zum Empfange der Gäste, zu den Festlichkeiten, zu außergewöhnlichen Gelegenheiten benützt werden. Da rufe man den Architekten, den Maler oder Bildhauer, den Decorateur herbei. Es wird schon Jeder denjenigen finden, den er verdient. Denn zwischen dem Producenten und dem Consumenten besteht ein geistiger Contact, der freilich für die Wohnräume nicht ausreichen kann.

So war es ja immer. Auch der König wohnte in einem Zimmer, das mit ihm und durch ihn geworden war. Aber seine Gäste empfing er in den vom Hofarchitekten geschaffenen Räumen. Und wenn dann die braven Unterthanen durch die goldenen Räume geführt wurden, dann entrang sich wol der braven Unterthanenbrust der Seufzer: „Ach hat's der gut! Wenn du doch auch so schön wohnen könntest!" Denkt sich doch der brave Unterthan den König nicht anders als im purpurnen Hermelinmantel mit dem Scepter in der Hand und der Krone auf dem Haupte spazierengehend. Was Wunder, wenn die braven Unterthanen sofort, sobald sie zu Gelde kamen, sich auch diese vermeintlichen königlichen Wohnräume anschafften. Hat's mich doch genug gewundert, daß ich noch nie Jemanden im Purpur herumlaufen sah.

Nach und nach haben wir auch zu unserm Schreck gesehen, daß der König sehr einfach wohnt, und da gab es denn auch einen plötzlichen Rückzug. Einfachheit, auch in den Festräumen, war Trumpf. In anderen Ländern ist man wieder im Vormarsche begriffen, während wir uns erst zum Rückzuge anschicken. Erspart kann nns dieser nicht werden, wie unsere Gewerbetreibenden — ach so gerne — glauben möchten. Geschmack und Lust an der Abwechslung sind immer verschwistert. Heute tragen wir enge Hosen, morgen weite und übermorgen wieder enge. Das weiß jeder Schneider. Ja, da könnten wir uns ja die Periode der weiten Hosen ersparen. O nein! Die brauchen wir, damit uns die engen Hosen wieder gefallen. Auch wir brauchen eine Periode der einfachen Festräume, um auf die reichen wieder vorbereitet zu werden. Wollen unsere Gewerbetreibenden die Einfachheit schneller überwinden, so gibt es nur Ein Mittel: sie müssen sie octroyiren.

Gegenwärtig aber fängt sie bei uns erst an. Das kann man wol am besten aus dem Umstande entnehmen, daß das meistbewunderte Zimmer in der Rotunde auch das einfachste ist. Ein Schlafzimmer mit Bad ist es. Hof-Tapezierer Schenzel hat es verfertigt, und es ist für denjenigen bestimmt, der es selbst *entworfen* hat. Ich glaube, das dies vielleicht den stärksten Reiz auf die sich stauenden Beschauer ausübt. Es übt den ganzen Zauber des Individuellen und Persönlichen aus. Niemand Anderer könnte darin wohnen, Niemand Anderer könnte es so voll und ganz auswohnen, erwohnen, wie der Besitzer selber, Otto Wagner.

Hofrath Exner hat das Zimmer sofort für die Pariser Weltausstellung erworben, wo es die Bestimmung haben wird, den Parisern eine fromme Täuschung vorzuführen, wie die Wiener schlafen und baden. Unter uns können wir uns ja eingestehen, daß wir noch weit davon entfernt sind. Aber eine große Umwandlung wird dieses Zimmer in unserem Wohnungswesen hervorrufen. Denn, wie ich schon früher hervorgehoben habe, den Leuten gefällt es. Das Oesterreichische Museum hat da durch seine Weihnachtsausstellung glücklich vorgearbeitet. Man denke nur, die Wiener finden jetzt sogar ein Messingbett schön. Kein reiches, sondern das einfachste, das man sich denken kann. Und dabei hat der Tapezierer nicht einmal den Versuch gemacht, die Messingstäbe durch Stoffe zu verleugnen, wie es bisher immer gang und gäbe war. Messingbetten mußten nämlich immer „gefüttert" werden. Ein glatte, grüngefärbte und polirte Wandvertäfelung umgibt das Zimmer, in die theilweise werthvolle Stiche eingelassen sind. Eine Ottomane mit einem Eisbärenfell, zwei Messingnachtkästchen, zwei Schränke und zwei Cabinette, ein Tisch mit zwei Fauteuils und einige Sessel füllen das Zimmer aus. Ueber der Wandvertäfelung sind naturalistische Kirschbaumzweige als Wandverkleidung gestickt. Ebenso ist auch das Velum über dem Bette decorirt. Der weißgetünchte Plafond hat im Kreise angeordnete, an Seidenschnüren hängende Glühlampen und demgemäß in Gyps modellirte Strahlen. Die farbige Wirkung, hervorgerufen durch das grüne Holz, das gelbe Messing, das weiße Fell und die rothen Kirschen ist eine außerordentliche. Ueber die Sessel dieses Zimmers zu sprechen, behalte ich mir noch vor. Aber für heute sei schon gesagt, daß der Teppich unrichtig ist. Die Rosenbeete, in denen wir früher herumsteigen mußten, haben wir gründlich abgethan. Ich glaube nicht, daß es angenehmer wirkt, durch den Teppich die Illusion erweckt zu bekommen, daß man über bloßgelegte Baumwurzeln stolpern könnte. Der Kirschenbaum sendet nämlich seine Wurzel über den ganzen Fußboden.

Ein Juwel ist auch das Bad. Die gesammte Wandverkleidung, der Fußbodenbelag, der Ottomanen-Ueberzug und die Pölster bestehen nämlich aus jenem wolligen Stoff, aus dem unsere Bademäntel verfertigt werden. Derselbe hat ein discretes violettes Muster erhalten, und dieses Weiß, Violett und Silber der vernickelten Möbel, der Toilette-Gegenstände und der Badewanne geben die Farbenstimmung an. Die Badewanne besteht nämlich aus Spiegelglas, das durch Nickel montirt wird. Sogar die Gläser auf dem Waschtisch — Facettenschliff — sind nach Wagner'schen Zeichnungen ausgeführt. Natürlich auch die reizende Toilette-Garnitur.

Ich bin ein Gegner jener Richtung, die etwas besonders Vorzügliches darin erblickt, daß ein Gebäude bis zur Kohlenschaufel aus der Hand eines Architekten hervorgehe. Ich bin der Meinung, daß dadurch das Gebäude ein sehr langweiliges Aussehen erhält. Jede Charakteristik geht dabei verloren. Aber vor dem Otto Wagner'schen Genius streiche ich die Segel. Otto Wagner hat nämlich eine Eigenschaft, die ich bisher nur bei wenigen englischen und amerikanischen Architekten gefunden habe: er kann nämlich aus seiner Architektenhaut hinaus- und in eine beliebige Handwerkerhaut hineinschlüpfen. Er macht ein Wasserglas — da denkt er wie ein Glasbläser und ein Glasschleifer. Er macht ein Messingbett — er denkt, er fühlt wie ein Messingarbeiter. Alles Uebrige, sein ganzes großes architektonisches Wissen und Können hat er in der alten Haut gelassen. Nur Eines nimmt er überall mit hinüber: seine Künstlerschaft. *Adolf Loos.*

Volkswohnungen.

Dicht neben dem Modell des herrlichen Palastes, welcher in Hinkunft den Wohnsitz unseres Kaisers bilden soll, hängen an einer der Wände des Stadterweiterungs-Pavillons ein paar Pläne, an denen wol die Meisten, geblendet durch den künstlerischen Glanz der übrigen Ausstellungsobjecte, vorübergehen, ohne sie zu sehen und zu beachten. Es sind die Pläne der Volkswohnhäuser, welche auf einem freien Platze nächst der Station Ottakring der Stadtbahn, von der „Kaiser-Franz-Josephs-Jubiläumsstiftung für Volkswohnungen und Wohlfahrtseinrichtungen" erbaut werden sollen. Und doch sollte Keiner, welcher der majestätischen Kunst den Tribut seiner Bewunderung gezollt, diese schlichte Ausstellung übersehen, denn sie bildet einen unerläßlichen Einklang in die Harmonie, die gerade in diesem Pavillon herrscht; Wien wird groß, wird wahrhaft schön, wird eine moderne Stadt nur sein, wenn es neben den glänzenden Ringstraßenpalästen auch wohnliche Heimstätten für das arme Volk, für den berühmten „kleinen Mann" besitzt; es soll sie besitzen, und was das Schönste ist, sie sollen aus derselben Quelle stammen, aus welcher die Mittel für den reichen Kaiserpalast stammen. Der Kaiser selbst hat aus dem Stadterweiterungsfonds eine Viertelmillion Gulden für die genannte Stiftung gewidmet, und es war daher ein sinnreicher Gedanke, ein Gedanke, der die Idee der socialen Versöhnung fördern muß, die Pläne für die ersten Volkswohnungen knapp neben dem Modell der neuen Hofburg den Ausstellungsbesuchern vor Augen zu führen.

Vor mehr als fünfunddreißig Jahren legte der bekannte amerikanische Philanthrop Peabody in seiner zweiten Vaterstadt London durch eine Millionenspende den Grund zu einer Stiftung, welche es auch dem Armen und Aermsten ermöglichen sollte, ein Heim zu besitzen, das nicht, wie die Massenquartiere der Londoner Elendsviertel, ein Grab für die physische und moralische Verfassung des Menschen wäre. Ein philanthropisches Genie, das Peabody war, suchte er den socialen Jammer der unteren Classen an den Wurzeln zu fassen und krönte sein reiches, im Dienste der Menschenliebe verbrachtes Lebenswerk durch eine Stiftung für Volkswohnungen. Die Peabody-Buildings sind heute das classische Vorbild für alle Schöpfungen ähnlicher Art; sie gewähren mehr als dreißigtausend Personen eine menschenwürdige Wohnung, den besten Arbeitern und Handwerkern Londons, die ohne diese Stiftung vielleicht weder an die Gründung einer Familie noch eines Gewerbes hätten denken können und in der klagenerfüllten Atmosphäre von Whitechapel körperlich und sittlich verkümmert wären. Wien ist auch eine Millionenstadt, aber es hatte bisher keinen Peabody. Allerdings dürfen wir mit stolzer Freude sagen, daß es in Wien auch kein Whitechapel gibt, aber was nicht ist, könnte leicht werden, wenn nicht rechtzeitig den gefährlichen Folgen einer unvermeidlichen Entwicklung vorgebeugt würde. Das Gespenst der Wohnungsnoth, welches sich an den Aufschwung der großen Städte heftet, geht auch bei uns erschreckend um; es gibt in Wien Bezirke, wo nur drei Percent der vorhandenen Wohnungen den allerbescheidensten Anforderungen der Hygiene und Sanitäts-Polizei entsprechen. Nicht weniger als 900,000 Menschen leben in Wien unter Verhältnissen, welche hygienisch eigentlich unzulässig sind; dicht neben den Stätten des glänzendsten Wohnungsüberflusses erheben sich die modernen Zinskasernen, wo bis zu zwanzig Miethparteien in engen, der Luft, des Lichtes und allen Anforderungen der Hygiene entbehrenden Quartieren zusammenwohnen, wo das Unwesen der Aftermiethe und der Bettgeher wuchert und wo gleichwol der Quadratmeter Wohnfläche erwiesenermaßen fast doppelt so viel kostet als in einer Ringstraßenwohnung. Welche materiellen und sittlichen Gefahren für die Gesammtheit nicht weniger als für den Einzelnen lauern an diesen Stätten des dichten Beisammenlebens? Die Wohnung ist nicht blos der Raum, wo ein Speisetisch und eine Ruhestätte Platz haben, sie ist auch der Tempel der Familie, der Sitz der Laren und Penaten, welche ebensoviele segnende Götter als quälende Dämonen werden können, je nachdem das „Heim" geschaffen ist. Je mehr der Kampf des täglichen Lebens der

> [It] has arrived. But not everywhere will it be greeted with enthusiasm. There may be many who have not felt any need for it at all. And many who imagined that it would be different. But one cannot deny that its appearance is an unassuming one. It has come for an exhibition, is staying outside the city in the Prater, and has promised in advance to leave in six months' time.[55]

Loos's assertion that the new style had arrived in the exhibition, he knew very well, was not wholly accurate. What becomes evident as one reads the full series of his reviews (which appeared weekly, in the Sunday editions of the newspaper) is that the new style was only infrequently to be found there. The task he set for himself was to discern for his audience what was modern at the exhibition and what was not – and, more tellingly, what it means to say that something *is* modern.

In the second of the essays, Loos explains to his audience how it was that he came to divorce himself from the historicist camp: "The bracing air of America and England has removed from me all prejudices about the products of my own time."[56] And he adds (as if he could not quite resist the temptation to irritate and exasperate) a rejoinder to his imagined critics, those who sought to preserve the old order.

> Unscrupulous people have tried to turn us against our own times. They have told us to look backwards, to take other ages as our models. Now, like a nightmare, it has passed for me. Yes indeed, our time is beautiful, so beautiful that I would not want to live in any other.[57]

But the spirit of the new age, Loos now discloses for the first time, is not universally present in the exhibits. It can be found only, he explains, in select places.

> In this age that is completely lacking in a crafts character of its own, two branches of our Austrian arts and crafts deserve great credit for having the strength of will not to join in with the general denial of our own times ... our producers of expensive leather goods and our gold- and silversmiths.[58]

Loos then proceeds to single out and applaud the specific forms and objects he thought conveyed the spirit and expression of the new style. He begins also to reveal the qualities he believed were coming to be essential: "simple lines," "restrained design," and "the awareness of the need to liberate ourselves from historical styles."[59]

Uniting all of these trends was what rested at the very heart of the modern for Loos: a continuous whittling away at the inessential. That which was superfluous was a lie or a sham, for modern life demanded absolute fealty to truth and simplicity. In the place of pretense and superfluity, Loos argues that the alternative is quality – quality of manufacture and quality of materials – all without adornment. In another of his early essays, "Die Herrenmode," (Men's Fashions) the men's fashions displayed at the exhibition, he introduces this view.

> Only a small number [of tailors] began with the idea of working in the most refined manner; most seek to please the dandies. And they have delighted [them] with double-buttoned vests, plaid suits, and velvet collars. One firm even went so far as to put blue velvet epaulets on a jacket. If *that* is not modern then what is?

Here, too, another of Loos's critical strategies makes its appearance: an acid and mocking wit. It is mostly lost in translation (or through the action of time, as the jokes have lost their meaning), but Loos's assaults on what he regards as the foibles of contemporary design are not infrequently invested with humor – always, of course, at the expense of those (or what) he is assailing. These witty remarks serve a purpose beyond a certain entertainment value. What Loos satirizes is always construed as an example of a cultural miscarriage. Always he presents its opposite, what in his view is correct and fitting. In design, there is the correct and modern way, and the misguided or inappropriate way. Loos's critiques are founded on such antinomies: authenticity versus pretense, art versus craft, simple versus overwrought. These pairings are for him ways of determining what is appropriate and what is not, what has value and what lacks it, what corresponds to the requirements and spirit of modern life and what runs counter to it, what features the new sensibility and what still embraces outmoded assumptions.

All of Loos's attempts to come to terms with what he sees around him are reliant upon his establishment of these categories. He makes meaning through a process of sorting, of determining which of these qualities something he sees has or lacks. Loosian disciple Paul Engelmann later wrote that Loos's intellectual and creative power issued from his ability "to separate and divide correctly," his winnowing out of "the detritus of once living cultural values" – of "combating 'inferior tendencies' posing as true heirs," while simultaneously searching for what could still be used.[60] For Loos, this was not a matter of formal invention. "New forms?," Engelmann quotes him as saying. "How dull! It is the new spirit that matters. Even out of old forms it will fashion what we new men need."[61]

To establish his categories, Loos needed to find answers to fundamental questions – questions that went to the heart of what it meant to design and live in a modern way. What he does is to generate a complex mental matrix of his categories. If this, then that. If not this, then not that. And each decision has multiple, cross-referencing parameters. Going through this imagined matrix then becomes for him a way to find answers to fundamental questions. Is something modern? Is it authentic? Does it serve a purpose – without pretense or unnecessary elaboration? In each instance, he must answer yes or no. The answers are also always weighted: some qualities, Loos decides, are more important than others.

The strategy had particular value for Loos because it allowed him to confront new and vexing problems. A fundamental one was whether history – and, by extension, historical models – still had any validity or use in the present. His response to this question is noteworthy, for it sets him apart from nearly all of the later modernists (who would reject the idea of direct historical models out of hand). He says, in another of his essays – one of his most important, on the products of the bronze industry – that there are, in fact, instances where history can serve us. "The solution," he writes, "to this burning question is: everything that was made in earlier centuries can be copied today, as long as it is still useful."[62]

He arrives at this answer because in his process of sorting the question of usefulness is more important than that of newness. And this is always true, he tells us, except in cases where the object did not previously exist: "New products of our culture (train cars, telephones, typewriters, and so on) must be formally conceived without a conscious recourse to already outmoded styles."[63] Loos, thus, is able to work out his answer on the basis of various conceptual pairings, which are set into the hierarchy he has established. The scheme enables him to form opinions swiftly and dependably. It also allows him to be extraordinarily consistent in his commentaries – and, subsequently, because he will follow the same method in arriving at design decisions, to be equally consistent as a practitioner.

In the hands of a lesser mind, such a system of thought might become stiff and unwieldy. But Loos shows himself, already very early on, capable of great nuance. In the same article on the bronze industry, for example, he appends one further thought, a key one, that will guide him ever after.

> What this means is either copy something completely or make something entirely new. By that, however, I do not mean that the new should be the opposite of that which came before.[64]

The second sentence contains what is perhaps one of his most luminous insights: even if one does not copy a past object, there are qualities in its design that might still have relevance in the present. What made an old chair comfortable, for instance, or how its structural requirements were solved, can yet offer us lessons. And such lessons retain their usefulness and meaning – even if the form or the style of the chair does not. This is so because fundamentally the problem of making a chair, as Loos would reiterate on multiple occasions, is not about aesthetics, but about how we sit.[65] Any other issues are secondary.

Central, then, to Loos's emerging theory is the primacy of functionality. But Loos is unwilling to stop there. Among the notable features of the Jubilee essays is that one can almost hear him thinking aloud. He establishes a principle in one or more of the early pieces, only to come back to it afterward in a subsequent essay and seek to refine it. In the case of functionality, Loos comes to understand that an object of daily use "serves" us in two ways: in the usual way, what we would describe as its "purpose" – which is to say very simply that something needs to serve its specific requirements well. For instance, a chair must be made in such a way that we can sit in it in comfort. Yet objects of daily use, he recognizes, also have another role: to contribute to people's lives, to their sense of identity and their emotions. An old chair may, for example, serve the purpose of remembrance: "That was my grandmother's chair," one might recall. The chair can "speak" to us about feelings of nostalgia – about the family and family tradition.

This is one reason why Loos was deeply skeptical about the professional designers of his time. He questioned whether academically trained architects understood the true meaning of functionality (falling instead prey to the sins of aestheticism, as the Secessionists, he was convinced, were doing); what they made was a form of artifice, detached from those they served.

> The "stylish" dwelling, this achievement of our century, requires an extreme amount of knowledge and ability.
>
> But that was not always the case. Until the turn of the century, this problem was unknown. One [simply] bought furniture from the cabinetmaker, wallpaper from the wallpaperer, and lighting from the bronze caster, and so on. But, surely, they wouldn't

> match exactly? Perhaps not, but that was not a consideration by which they were guided. In those days, people furnished their rooms in the same way we dress today. We get our shoes from the shoemaker, jacket, trouser, and vest from the tailor, collar and cuffs from the shirt manufacturer, hat from the hat maker, walking stick from the wood turner. Not one of them knows the other, and yet all the things go together. Why? Because they all work in the style of 1898. And that also is how craftsmen in the furnishing industry used to work in former times, all following a common style, the then current, modern style.[66]

The turn away from traditional practices of making interiors had come about, Loos writes, when the furnishing of apartments was given over to architects, who were "well versed in the specialist literature" and therefore able to carry out any commission "in any style."[67] But such spaces were neither cozy – another of Loos's categorical imperatives – nor did they express the real tastes or outlooks of their owners. He calls for a revolution, a move away from such structured and determined spaces.

> We want to be the lords of our own four walls again. If we lack taste, then so be it; we will decorate tastelessly. If we have good taste, all the better. But we refuse to be tyrannized by our own rooms any longer. We will buy everything together, everything that we will eventually need, and what we like.[68]

There is manifesto-like quality to his statement, as if Loos, now gaining ever more confidence in his opinions, is announcing his willingness to lead a popular movement. And this movement, as he makes patent, is against the tyranny of style (regardless of whether it is old or new), against the tyranny of the architects and academically trained designers.

It is also less obviously, although no less vitally, against the concept of "completeness." For Loos, increasingly as he develops his thoughts in the Jubilee essays over the course of that summer and fall, comes to argue the idea that all interiors are works in progress. They change as the circumstances of their owners change, as the needs and perceptions of their owners evolve. Moreover, they reflect, in a profound way, the family and its history.

> I did not, thank God, grow up in a stylish apartment. In those days, they were unknown. Unfortunately, that is no longer the case for my family. But in those days! There was the table, a crazy curlicue thing, an extendable table, with some dreadful metalwork. But it was *our* table, *our* table! Can you imagine what that meant? Can you imagine what splendid hours we spent at it? By lamplight! In the evening, when I was a little boy, I couldn't tear myself away from it; my father had to keep imitating the sound of the watchman's horn so that I would run off in fright to the nursery. And there was the writing desk. There was an ink stain on it. My sister Hermine spilled the ink on it when she was a tiny baby. And there were the pictures of my parents. What terrible frames! But they were a wedding gift from father's workmen. And the old-fashioned chair over there. A left-over from my grandmother's house. ... Every piece of furniture, every object, every thing had a story to tell, the story of our family. Our home was never finished. It changed with us, and we with it. There was certainly no style in it. Which is to say no alien style, no old style. But the apartment did have style, the style of those who lived within, the style of my family.[69]

The idea that an interior is never finished is a remarkably potent one – even today. It was, at the time, certainly a novel one. It hints at both the possibilities of a new, modern eclecticism and the principle of continuous making, of continuous design. Decisions about what comes into or goes out of the interior happen in the moment; such actions are forever directed toward what is required and desired by the occupants.

But if one reads the Jubilee exhibition essays with care, it is evident that Loos is not advocating a form of design anarchy. He assumes that if the system works as it should, and craftspeople are making objects that reflect the spirit of the moment, then the pieces that families acquire and the interiors they assemble will exhibit the same inherent contemporaneousness: they will all be "modern." Modern for Loos is never a simple matter, however. It is not bound up with style but, rather, with culture. The challenge for the maker (or designer), he believed, is to discern where the culture is, and to produce objects, spaces, or buildings accordingly. This, he was convinced, did not entail the need to contrive something – to create it *ex nihilo*. His expressed modus is about responding to what is happening more broadly and finding solutions that match the spirit of the times. And such design adjustments to a changing culture, he thought, in some cases might be merely incremental.

Loos was sure that he could see the cultural trends of his day and predict what would come. He elucidates this idea powerfully in one of the most well-known essays of the series, "Das Luxusfuhrwerk," (Luxury Carriages), which was published in early July. Ostensibly, it is about the differences between English and Austrian carriage design. But he introduces for the first time the theme that was to eclipse all others in his writings – his attack on ornament.

> Let us merely recall a few chapters of cultural history. The less advanced a nation is, the more lavish its ornament, its decoration. The Indian covers every object, every boat, every oar, every arrow, wholly and completely, with ornament. To prefer ornament is to put oneself at the level of the Indian. But we must seek to overcome the Indian in us. ... The goal towards which the whole of mankind is striving is to see beauty in form alone, and not to make it dependent on ornament and decoration.[70]

The fundamental ingredients of Loos's famed later essay "Ornament und Verbrechen" (Ornament and Crime, 1910) are already present here: the notions that the trajectory of cultural history is leading away from ornament and that the continued use of ornament in modern times is atavistic.[71] These ideas would become part of his theoretical stock in trade, and he would come to repeat them many times.

The other key concepts in the piece – the import of craft, the idea of a liberation from the architect and designer, the repudiation of carefully tuned styles in dwelling (which is to say, the *Gesamtkunstwerk*, or total work of art) – he had already introduced in his previous essays. They are also echoed in the review articles he wrote afterward.

Two of his other principal ideas come into view in his later writings in 1898, one having to do with the problem of fashion, the other relating once more to tradition. Of fashion, Loos's commentary speaks to its social consequences. And it does so in two ways. On the one hand, he argues in his article "Damenmode" (Women's Fashions) – which was published in August but was not included with the Jubilee exhibition essays – against the sensuality and confining nature of women's fashions, because he understands such clothing as an impediment to women's liberation.

> We are heading toward a newer, better age. Women will no longer have to appeal to sensuality to achieve equal status with men, but they will do so through their economic and intellectual independence, gained through work. A woman's value will not rise and fall with fluctuations in sensuality. Silks and satins, flowers and frills, feathers and colors will lose their effectiveness. They will disappear. (And rightly so. In our culture, there is no place for them.)[72]

Women's fashions – and, indeed, fashion in general – Loos sees as a byproduct of a cultural outlook, and because the culture was rapidly shifting (and the value of women along with it), so, too, according to him, would fashion. In several of the essays, he makes comments about the practicality of clothing, the need for it to allow both women and men to move about freely (one of his definitions of modern life has to do with free movement of the body) and to be comfortable in their clothing.

Loos makes one other comment that would become crucial for him and his theories: that fashion also has significant economic implications, especially for its makers. In the essay on shoemakers, he drives this idea home.

> Our shoemakers happen to be capable men. They are filled with great spirit and individuality. ... This is all the more surprising as our shoemakers are poorly paid for their efforts. The public is forcing down the prices more and more, and the discrepancy, if the tradesman does not want to go out of business, is made up in the shoes themselves. Do not imagine that the shoemaker gets any pleasure out of being compelled to produce poor work. But you are forcing him to do so.[73]

The problem Loos sees is again twofold. Shoemakers were losing the joy of work by having to make poor-quality shoes in order to meet the demand for inexpensive shoes, because of the competition brought about by the factory. This was also harming the shoemakers in another way: because of their increasing exploitation, they were experiencing a loss of social status. Thus, they could no longer find joy in their work (a notion that Loos almost certainly took over from John Ruskin and, even more, William Morris). Loos would come back to this idea in subsequent writings (in "Ornament and Crime," for example) and describe with increased vigor the deleterious impact of industrialization on craftpeople. But the germ of his social critique was already formed by this time.

The last of the Jubilee exhibition essays, those he penned in the early autumn (on such diverse topics as underwear and books), were mostly an extension of the thoughts he had already forged. His main intellectual work behind him, he began to apply his critical ideas with ever greater precision. And he would do so long afterward. Over the coming years, he would continue to write – until 1902, he was still writing more than he was designing – and he would polish and upgrade his theories even after that. Some of his most important essays – "Die Überflüssigen" (The Superfluous Ones, 1908), "Lob der Gegenwart" (In Praise of the Present, 1908), "Ornament und Verbrechen" (Ornament and Crime, 1910), and "Architektur" (Architecture, 1910) – were still a decade or more off in the future. But everything he wrote after 1898 was a direct outcome of the Jubilee exhibition essays. After the turn of the century, when he began working in earnest, first as a designer and then as an architect, what he created was a consequence of the basic notions he had laid out in the essays.

He made and built what he wrote, and with an astonishing constancy that would persist to his last days.

2 | The Origins and Meanings of "Ornament and Crime"

Adolf Loos's famed polemic "Ornament and Crime" ("Ornament und Verbrechen") holds a special place in his work. Almost one hundred years after its composition, it remains the best known of Loos's writings and one of the most often read and cited discourses on modern design. It is also generally regarded as the defining essay of Loos's ideology, the requisite text for unraveling his idiosyncratic approach to building and design. Yet its origins and context have been surprisingly little studied, and Loos's intentions and the essay's broader meanings have been consistently misunderstood or misrepresented.

In his article on Loos in the *Macmillan Encyclopedia of Architects*, published in 1982, Carter Wiseman succinctly summed up what for many years was the conventional view of "Ornament and Crime."

> In his writings, Loos came increasingly to focus on what he regarded as the excesses of decoration in both traditional design and in the more recent products of the Vienna Secession and the Wiener Werkstätte. Loos expressed his irritation most strongly in "Ornament and Crime," a short essay published in 1908 that flew in the face of contemporary practice ... The essay caused a furor

Adolf Loos, ca. 1912. Wien Museum, Vienna.

Adolf Loos (left), Karl Kraus (center), and Herwarth Walden (right) in Vienna, late October 1909. Kraus introduced Loos to Walden, who organized the architect's presentation of an early version of "Ornament and Crime" on November 11, 1909 at Paul Cassirer's gallery in Berlin. Karl Kraus Collection, Special Collections and Archives, University of Massachusetts at Amherst University Library.

> and was widely circulated abroad (Le Corbusier referred to it as "an Homeric cleansing of architecture"). It rapidly became a key document in the modernist literature.[1]

The same set of "facts" has been consistently reproduced – with little variation – in almost every account of "Ornament and Crime" from the 1930s to the present day. For decades, scholars writing about Loos have reported that he penned the essay in 1908, and many have stated that he first published the essay in 1908 or 1910, without citing where it appeared.[2] In fact, the story of the essay's genesis and its publication history turns out to have been quite different. And the confusion and myths about the essay concern not only when it was written and when and where it was published. Another persistent myth has to do with the purported reception of "Ornament and Crime." Most accounts since the 1930s have described a "riotous" reaction on the part of the public and withering criticism from the Viennese establishment. Again, the truth turns out to have been far more varied and nuanced – and it reveals much about the contemporary situation in Vienna. Scholars have also been unclear or incorrect about who or what were Loos's targets, how and why he came to write the piece, the precise sources of his ideas, and the larger context in which the essay appeared.[3] More recently, Loos has also come under attack "because of the racist and misogynist descriptions that sit so boldly on [the essay's] surface."[4] Some have assailed Loos – unfairly – for single-handedly bringing about the demise of ornament – or, at least, for failing to recognize its significance.

A careful exploration of the surviving evidence and of the period around 1910 offers a clearer view not only of how Loos came to write the text and what his aims were but how the various myths later arose. It reveals the close relationship between Loos's writings and his design work, and how the changing climate of professional and public opinion would drive him to expound his ideas. Despite Loos's efforts to articulate his views, the essay would take on a life of its own and lead to consequences he neither foresaw nor desired.

The Genesis of "Ornament and Crime" and the First Berlin Lecture

More than two decades ago, in his article "Ornament und Mythos," Burkhardt Rukschcio, who along with Roland L. Schachel produced what has become the standard monograph on Loos, *Adolf Loos: Leben und Werk*, sought to set the record straight about the genesis of "Ornament and Crime."[5] Rukschcio, drawing on new sources, contended that Loos first presented it as a public talk in Vienna on January 21, 1910 under the auspices of the Akademischer Verband für Literatur und Musik (Academic Association for Literature and Music) and that Loos read from a fully developed manuscript. A newspaper report confirms that Loos did present a lecture in Vienna in late January, and a surviving manuscript that Rukschcio discovered contains internal references suggesting that it was probably the text Loos read that day.[6]

But new evidence reveals that the story is far more complex: while Loos's presentation of "Ornament and Crime" in Vienna was the first delivery of the full talk as we know it now, many elements of the piece were already contained in a lecture he presented the previous November; in all likelihood, the carefully written-out manuscript of 1910 was a later, more fully elaborated version of the 1909 talk.

The first clue to unraveling the mystery of "Ornament and Crime" appears in an article in October 1910 about the controversy surrounding Loos's building on the Michaelerplatz in Vienna for the tailoring firm Goldman & Salatsch. Loos had begun work on the building the previous year, and construction had commenced in the spring of 1910.[7] By late September, the exterior walls were complete and the building had been plastered. The effect of the plain white upper stories (the stone veneer on the lower portion would not be installed until the following year) was stridently modern, prompting one local newspaper, the *Neuigkeits-Welt-Blatt*, to compare it to a grain elevator. The article also noted that it was Loos's intention to leave the building unornamented, although this was not entirely true.[8] Almost immediately, a public controversy erupted, prompting the Vienna municipal building authorities to suspend the building permit. An article in one of the Berlin newspapers, reporting on the situation, noted: "The architect is the well-known art-'modernist' Adolf Loos, who delivered a much commented-upon lecture 'Ornament and Crime' last year in Berlin."[9]

Loos had in fact presented a lecture in Berlin in November 1909, although it was advertised under a different name: "Kritik der angewandten Kunst" (Critique of Applied Art). The lecture took place in the gallery of the art dealer Paul Cassirer, at Viktoriastraße 35, in Tiergarten, close to Potsdamer Platz.

Cassirer had founded the gallery with his cousin Bruno Cassirer in 1898. It soon became a leading outlet for the works of the Berlin Secessionists, including Max Liebermann and Max Slevogt. Cassirer also played a prominent role in promoting Vincent van Gogh, Paul Cézanne, and other French Impressionists and post-Impressionists, and, beginning in 1907, he began publishing the writings of young German modernists, among them Else Lasker-Schüler, Heinrich Mann, Carl Sternheim, Ernst Toller, and Frank Wedekind.[10]

The organizer of Loos's lecture in Berlin, however, was not Cassirer but the composer, art dealer, and publisher Herwarth Walden (see fig. 2.1). Born Georg Lewin, in 1878, Walden had studied composition and piano in Berlin and Florence. During the early years of the century, he wrote modern *Lieder.* But he is best known as the founder of the Expressionist magazine *Der Sturm*, which he launched in 1910, and for his role in discovering and promoting many young, still-unknown artists.[11] Loos had met Walden through his close friend, the Viennese satirist Karl Kraus.[12] In April 1909, Walden had taken over the directorship of the biweekly magazine *Das Theater*, and in June of the same year, during a trip to Vienna, he approached Kraus about writing for the journal. It was then that he met Loos.[13] Loos and Kraus recognized in Walden a kindred spirit, and both men began regularly corresponding with him.

It is unclear from their surviving letters whether Loos first suggested giving a talk in Berlin or whether the idea came from Walden, but it is almost certain that it was Walden who went to Cassirer to make the arrangements.[14] The first direct evidence of the preparations is in a telegram from Loos, dated September 9, 1909, addressed to both Walden and the "Kunst-Salon Cassirer" confirming the date: November 11, 1909.[15] At the time, Loos did not have a title for the talk. In a note appended to a letter Kraus sent to Walden a little more than a week later, Loos writes: "I ... hope to send you a title for my lecture in the next several days. Up to now, I have come up with: 'Critique of So-called Applied Art.' If you have no objection to this 'tapeworm,' then so be it."[16]

Loos undoubtedly discussed the details of the talk with Walden when the latter visited Vienna from October 23 to 25. A little more than a week later, Kraus wrote to Walden confirming that he, too, would come to Berlin to attend the lecture, and that he and Loos would travel by train together as far as Dresden on the day of the talk. Loos would make a stopover in Dresden for a few hours to prepare, and would arrive at the Anhalter Station in Berlin at five in the evening, only three hours before he was scheduled to speak.[17]

The official sponsor of the event was the Verein für Kunst (Association for Art), a group Walden had founded. He had patterned it after the Vienna Verein für Kunst und Kultur (Association for Art and Culture), an organization to which both Loos and Kraus belonged that organized performances of modern music and readings by avant-garde authors.[18] Announcements of Loos's lecture appeared in at least two Berlin newspapers on the day of the presentation, but in all likelihood Walden and Cassirer invited most of those who attended.[19] Loos was not yet well known in Berlin; even in Vienna, prior to the Michaelerplatz commission, his reputation was based largely on his writings for the newspapers and a few small projects, mostly notably the interior for the Café Museum (1899) and the Kärntner Bar (1908–9).[20] It was not until the controversy surrounding the Goldman & Salatsch Building erupted the following year that he would be thrust fully into the public spotlight.

No manuscript or notes for Loos's November 11, 1909 presentation are known to have survived. Newspaper reports, however, provide some clues about what he said and how his ideas were received. The *Berliner Börsen-Courier* reported that Loos spoke in a "riveting" Viennese dialect, and commented that his theories were not developed in a "systematic" fashion. The particular target of his critique, the anonymous reporter noted, was the tendency of designers to produce objects of daily use (Gebrauchsgegenstände). But "art and craft," the reviewer quotes Loos as saying, "should be completely divorced from each other."[21] A review in the *Berliner Lokal-Anzeiger* offered a very similar account: Loos "wants the emancipation of handicraft, he wants it left to 'its own natural instincts,' as these have been preserved for centuries. With much hot air and great energy, he assailed the meddling of artists in purely practical and private matters."[22]

None of these ideas were new for Loos: he had been voicing such criticisms since before the turn of the century, and he published them on repeated occasions. But a few lines in the two reviews stand out. Both quote a key line from Loos: "The evolution of culture is synonymous with the removal of ornament from objects of daily use."[23]

This is, of course, one of the central passages in "Ornament and Crime," as the essay was later published.[24] There is little else in the two reviews, however, that brings to mind the published text of "Ornament and Crime." Yet Loos later referred to this talk as "Ornament and Crime" in the letter he wrote to Walden a little less than a year later, discussing his forthcoming lecture "Über Architektur" (On Architecture). Loos also provided Walden with a plainly worded advertisement for the newspapers: "Architect Adolf Loos is already well known to us through his lecture of the previous year, 'Ornament and Crime,' which aroused so much controversy."[25] This announcement must have been the source for the reference to Loos's 1909 Berlin lecture that appeared in the *Berliner Lokal-Anzeiger* in October 1910.[26]

Two of Loos's assertions raise questions: that he gave the lecture "the previous year," and that the lecture "aroused so much controversy." The newspaper accounts from 1909 seem to refute Loos's claim of a controversy. The review in the *Berliner Börsen-Courier*, though somewhat critical, is polite and makes no mention of any hostility on the part of the audience.[27] The reporter for the *Berliner Lokal-Anzeiger* writes that "at the end of the lecture there was a question and answer session that brought much that was interesting to light, and the speaker, in addition to friendly applause, also received a few jeers."[28] But this hardly suggests the sort of contentious reception that Loos described.

That the audience was mostly receptive to Loos's message can be readily explained. Cassirer's gallery was not very large; there would likely have been no more than thirty or forty people in attendance. Many were undoubtedly friends or acquaintances of either Walden or Cassirer and therefore likely to be favorably disposed to Loos's ideas. From the surviving correspondence, however, it is clear that Loos hoped very much to generate a controversy. In the last line of his note to Walden in September 1909 concerning a possible title, he writes: "The title must be phrased in such a way that the applied artists will come in."[29] Loos wanted to confront the traditional applied artists in Berlin and to demonstrate why their approach was misguided. It is possible that he altered the title to the familiar "Ornament and Crime" at the last minute, though there is no record of this. In the end, he must have been disappointed that the lecture failed to arouse more of a stir. The lines he penned for the advertisement he sent to Walden the following autumn suggest that he wanted to foster the illusion that the earlier lecture had been a larger and more important event than appears to have been the case. Loos's instructions to Walden for advertising his lecture reveal his desire to avoid the sort of tepid response he had received in 1909: he asked Walden to make sure that "all of the Charlottenburger architecture students" – i.e., those at the Berlin Technische Hochschule (Technical University) – "are invited with a billboard" and to make sure that the architecture professors at the school receive announcements by mail.[30]

Loos's claim that he presented "Ornament and Crime" in Berlin in November 1909 is more difficult to explain. He spoke again in Berlin in early March 1910, this time under the title "Ornament und Verbrechen," and it is possible that he was confused about the dates. But it is more likely, given the short time that had elapsed, that he understood "Kritik der angewandten Kunst," as he had presented it in November 1909, to be a version of "Ornament and Crime."

There is no evidence that Loos prepared a text for his 1909 Berlin talk. He apparently spoke freely or from notes. This seems to be confirmed by the two newspaper reviews of the presentation, which suggest that Loos's lecture lacked clear organization. Later in life, in the 1920s and 1930s, Loos usually presented lectures without relying on a written text. His third wife, Claire Beck Loos, recalled that he preferred to improvise when speaking publicly: "Never have I prepared for a lecture," she quotes him as saying. "I always improvise at the last minute. It would be impossible for me to read a lecture from notes."[31] But the existence of a number of lecture texts from his earlier years, including "Ornament and Crime" and "Mein Haus am Michaelerplatz" (My Building on the Michaelerplatz), contradicts this assertion.[32] Indeed, in the period before World War I, Loos appears to have used various approaches, sometimes reading from prepared texts, sometimes reading written passages while also improvising, and occasionally speaking entirely freely. He may not have recalled fully what he said in 1909, remembering a lecture that was closely related to the final version of "Ornament and Crime."

What undoubtedly contributed to Loos's confusion was his tendency to recycle older material. As a number of scholars have noted, many of the ideas and images in "Ornament and Crime" appear in his earlier writings.[33] In "Die Überflüssigen (Deutscher Werkbund)" (The Superfluous Ones [The German Werkbund], 1908), for example, is a passage that directly presages the core ideas of "Ornament and Crime": "The decoration of objects of daily use marks the beginning of art. The Papuan covers all of his household articles with ornament. The history of humanity shows how art sought to free itself from being profaned by emancipating itself from making objects of daily use, from the products of ordinary craftspeople."[34] Loos's close friends and others writing about him in this period also make similar allusions. Kraus repeatedly referenced Loos's anti-ornament ideas in his publication *Die Fackel* before November 1909, and many of the basic premises of what would become "Ornament and Crime" are succinctly summarized in the journalist Robert Scheu's sketch of Loos, which appeared in *Die Fackel* in the summer of 1909.[35]

One could indeed argue that Loos had been working on "Ornament and Crime" for more than a decade before he wrote the version we now know. He began to formulate his attitude toward ornament even before he returned from his nearly three-year-long sojourn in the United States in 1896. His first explicit assault on ornament came in his article on luxury carriages "Das Luxusfuhrwerk," which was published in the *Neue Freie Presse* in 1898.[36] Over the next decade, as his writings demonstrate, he gradually added the various features of his argument.[37]

"Ornament and Crime" bears some parallels with Loos's published essays of 1908, "Kultur" (Culture), "Lob der Gegenwart" (In Praise of the Present Day), and "Die Überflüssigen," and these have led Rukschcio and Schachel to argue that it belongs to this group of texts.[38] There is no evidence for this, however. The three essays were written for the Munich literary and cultural magazine *März*, edited by Ludwig Thoma, Hermann Hesse, Albert Langen, and Kurt Aram, and all were considerably shorter, running only two or three pages.[39] Another of Loos's essays of this period, "Kulturentartung" (Cultural Degeneration), which is of similar length, was probably also written for *März*, but it was not published until 1931 in Loos's *Trotzdem*, a compilation of his essays spanning the years from 1900 to 1930.[40] "Ornament and Crime," on the other hand, is considerably longer – more than twice the length of the other essays – and its tone is very different, at once more strident, pensive, and rhetorical.

The First Vienna Lecture

What is certain is that Loos presented "Ornament and Crime" as a lecture in Vienna on January 21, 1910, a little more than two months after his first Berlin talk.

The Akademischer Verband für Literatur und Musik was the official sponsor for the event. It had been founded by Viennese students in 1908 and was the only organization in the city – aside from the related Verein für Kunst und Kultur – that regularly sponsored avant-garde art, literature, and music.[41] The critic Oskar Maurus Fontana observed that it was at the Verband "where the ... most searching intellects gathered."[42] The group organized Kraus's first public lecture, and it put on readings by Egon Friedell, Frank Wedekind, Stefan Zweig, and other modern writers. In the decade before the war, the organization was also avid in its support of composer Arnold Schönberg and his disciples Alban Berg and Anton von Webern, who experienced intense hostility from the Viennese critics and much of the public.[43] The group's membership was composed mostly of students, artists, and the city's young literati and culturati. When Loos spoke in early 1910, the great majority of the audience would have been made up of those who regularly attended its lectures and performances.

The exact location of the lecture is unknown. The Akademischer Verband often rented the Sophiensaal on the Marxergasse in the third district, which seated nearly 2,700 for larger events, but Loos's talk was probably held in the adjacent Kleiner Saal, which it used for smaller lectures and concerts.

Only one report of the event has come to light, in the Vienna newspaper *Fremden-Blatt*. The unsigned review offers a few surprises. The reporter mentions that the lecture lasted "barely a half hour," and castigates Loos for being a less-than-scintillating speaker: "Adolf Loos is not a speaker in the usual sense; his lecture was lacking somewhat in ornament, in rhetorical accompaniment."[44] The reporter also mentions that the lecture was accompanied by "many topical slides" and that Loos received "loud applause" at the end. Afterward, there was "an often very animated discussion," but one that "for the most part did not extend much beyond superfluous banter" (müßige Timpeleien).[45]

Once more, Loos apparently failed to arouse much controversy. Given the audience, this is hardly surprising. Most of those present would have been sympathetic to modernism, and many would have already been familiar with his anti-ornament views from his writings or his architectural tours.[46] Undoubtedly, a number of his friends and acquaintances were in the audience; another sizable group probably in attendance that night were architecture students from the Technische Hochschule or the Akademie der bildenden Künste (Academy of Fine Arts), many of whom had encountered Loos in the coffeehouses and heard his impromptu talks.[47]

The *Fremden-Blatt* review includes an extensive summary of Loos's lecture, quoting key sentences and phrases. Most of the main theses of the later, published version are cited, confirming that this was very likely the first complete presentation of "Ornament and Crime," as we know it. The reporter recorded faithfully Loos's assertion that the "evolution of culture is synonymous with the removal of ornament from objects of daily use," his arguments concerning the exploitative elements of modern ornament, and his opening comments about the erotic origins of art.[48] But it is also certain that Loos did not merely read the text. A straight reading of "Ornament and Crime," as it was later published, would take only about fifteen to twenty minutes, even at a leisurely pace, meaning that Loos must have spoken ad lib, probably referring to the slides and elaborating his thoughts.

Loos very likely first wrote out the original text of "Ornament and Crime" in December 1909 or early January 1910. He spent the first three weeks of December in Vienna. From the little remaining evidence, it appears that he was working during this period on the design of the Goldman & Salatsch Building. On December 23, he left to spend the Christmas holidays with his common-law wife, Bessie Bruce, who was being treated for tuberculosis at a sanatorium in Leysin, in the Swiss Alps.[49] Loos returned briefly to Vienna around New Year's Day, but left a few days later for Leysin, this time traveling with the young artist Oskar

Kokoschka. Loos arranged for Kokoschka to stay at the sanatorium to paint portraits of some of the patients.[50] It is unclear when Loos returned to Vienna, but it was probably after January 10. Whether he wrote out the manuscript over the next ten days or so or in the few weeks beforehand is unknown.

We do know a little about Loos's state of mind in this period. Sometime in December or early January, he had shown a model of the Goldman & Salatsch Building to the architect Robert Oerley and the critic Richard Schaukal, as well as the two clients, Leopold Goldman and his brother-in-law Emanuel Aufricht.[51] The model, which no longer exists, apparently displayed the upper stories with little or no applied ornament. Oerley wrote a short time later in the *Jahrbuch der Gesellschaft österreichischer Architekten* that he thought that the building "promised to be something good." But he also noted that "in the beginning, there will be a great deal of criticism."[52] Schaukal, too, told Loos that he thought he would face a bitter fight with public opinion.[53] Their reactions may have made Loos aware for the first time that controversy might erupt in the coming year.

Loos was undeterred, however, and the stridency of "Ornament and Crime" suggests that he had resolved to promote his anti-ornament agenda in the public arena, come what may. The surviving manuscript, described by Rukschcio in "Ornament und Mythos," is most probably the text he read that night.[54] The principal clue comes from the passage in which Loos details the differences in cultural development among the Austrian empire's citizenry: "The speed of cultural development is retarded by stragglers. I may be living in the year 1910, but my neighbor lives around 1900 and the fellow over there in 1880."[55] The fact that Loos uses the date 1910 for his own day in what appears to be the original manuscript of the talk confirms that the date of composition must have been around this time. In subsequent versions, Loos changed the date, first to 1911, then to 1912, and, finally, in what was apparently his last public version of the talk, to 1913.

The Misdating of "Ornament and Crime"

The 1908 date was assigned to the text only much later. Franz Glück, who in the early 1960s assembled a complete edition of Loos's writings, *Adolf Loos: Sämtliche Schriften in zwei Bänden*, explained in the book's afterword how the work came to be published, thereby offering clues to how the misdating likely occurred.[56] The first appearance of the 1908 dating came in 1929, when "Ornament and Crime" was printed in the *Frankfurter Zeitung*.[57] Glück and Heinrich

Kulka, who was then working as Loos's assistant, had begun to collect Loos's scattered writings. Their goal was to publish a collection of his later texts, which appeared in 1931 under the title *Trotzdem*. Glück, who was an unnamed contributor to the book, and Kulka assembled the texts and made a number of "stylistic improvements." It was they who assigned the dates to many of Loos's manuscripts, including "Ornament and Crime," which they published in the *Frankfurter Zeitung* on October 24, 1929 in what is now the standard version of the text. But there were a number of problems, as Glück writes, with it and Loos's other manuscripts.

> Already at that time when *Trotzdem* appeared, Loos no longer had any recollection of many of his essays. He had never considered that he might assemble a small archive or catalogue of his written works. His dating [of the essays], which were preserved only in manuscript form and which in many cases were fragmentary – some had been lost entirely – [and] any indication of where the pieces had been published, was entirely unsure. It was not the time then to reexamine [the dating], but also our trust in what we found was too great.[58]

The essay, as it appeared in the *Frankfurter Zeitung*, had a brief foreword, probably based on information from Loos. It begins: "This article dates from the year 1908."[59] When the essay was published in *Trotzdem* two years later, it also bore the 1908 date. Kulka and Glück may have erred in dating the essay because of something they saw in Loos's papers, or Loos, when asked, may have misremembered the date or assigned it to 1908 in order to establish his early role in the rejection of ornament. What is certain is that the editors changed the year in the passage about cultural development to 1908 ("I may live in the year ... ") and dated the essay the same year. This is how it appeared in every subsequent version – until recently, when some editors and writers, responding to Rukschcio's article, began assigning the 1910 date.[60]

Loos's Intentions

The dating of the essay is more than a matter of scholarly pedantry: it goes to the heart of the question of why and for whom Loos wrote it. Here again, the original manuscript offers important clues. In the later, published version, Loos attacks by name three prominent designers of the time: Otto Eckmann, Henry van de Velde, and Joseph Maria Olbrich. In the original manuscript, as Rukschcio noted, Josef Hoffmann is also mentioned (Loos describes him as the "Künstler [artist] Hoffmann"), but Loos subsequently removed this passage.[61]

Eckmann was the easiest target. He had been among the most prominent designers of the "florid" phase of the Jugendstil around the turn of the century, contributing graphic work for the magazines *Pan* and *Jugend* and creating two of the most popular fonts in the new style, *Eckmann* and *Fette Eckmann*. But Eckmann died in 1902, and by 1910 his work appeared very dated – exactly the point Loos wanted to make.[62]

Loos's attack on the other designers is more problematic. All three had continued to work through the early years of the century, but their designs had begun to evolve in new directions: Olbrich found his way back to neoclassicism before he died in 1908; and Van de Velde and Hoffmann had, by 1910, started to adopt new stylistic ideas, in Hoffmann's case, Biedermeier neoclassicism, in Van de Velde's, a simpler idiom based on pure geometries. All three continued to employ applied ornament, however, and it was on these grounds that Loos found them suitable targets.

The assertion many later commentators have made, that "Ornament and Crime" is an attack specifically on the Jugendstil, is not exactly correct.[63] Loos's aim was to disparage not a specific stylistic approach, but the use of modern ornament altogether. He was very much aware that new design directions were emerging at the time and that the Jugendstil was waning. What troubled him was that Hoffmann and the other designers had continued to embrace the idea that an invented ornamental language had a place in modern design – and that they continued to regard themselves as artists.

This distinction between the designer as artist or as craftsman was one of the fundamental divisions in Viennese modernist circles, and it is central to Loos's writings. As early as 1898, in an article in the periodical *Dekorative Kunst*, he had sought to distinguish his approach from that of Hoffmann and the other "artist designers": "It is difficult for me to write about Josef Hoffmann, for I am utterly opposed to the direction being taken today by young artists, and not only in Vienna. For me tradition is everything – the free working of the imagination takes second place."[64] (Hoffmann countered Loos's attack a few years later in his essay "Einfache Möbel": "Were we going to have the old craft tradition? God forbid."[65])

The controversy between the two men intensified after Hoffmann, together with Koloman Moser and textile manufacturer Fritz Waerndorfer, founded the

Wiener Werkstätte in 1903. From the start, Loos regarded the Wiener Werkstätte as a decided step backward. Rather than embracing the spirit of the new age, he was convinced that the Werkstätte's products further confused the differences between the spheres of art and craft. "Previously at least," he wrote in 1907 about one of Hoffmann's designs for a gridded metal jardinière, "a trace of what might be called applied art was evident, but now the grid of our manhole covers is being used for the décor of flower pots and fruit bowls."[66]

Such objections form the core of "Die Überflüssigen," Loos's critique of the German Werkbund, from 1908. He concludes the essay with an argument against the notion of the artist-designer: "What we need is a 'cabinetmakers' culture.' If the applied artists were to go back to painting pictures or sweeping the streets, we would have one."[67] Loos's "Kritik der angewandten Kunst" of the following year (in which, as one reviewer recorded, he attacked with particular vehemence reformers "like Riemerschmidt [*sic*] and Van de Velde") and the later, full version of "Ornament and Crime" were escalations of this ongoing assault on applied art.[68] After failing to arouse the vocal response he had hoped for, he made his critique even more pointed, equating the ambitions of applied artists with criminality.

Ornament and Crime

For Loos, the close pairing of ornament and crime was more than an adroit metaphor. He regarded the making of ornament by those who should have known better – architects and designers working in Vienna and the other Central European art centers after the turn of the century – as a deeply antisocial act. "The person of our time," he writes, "who from inner compulsion smears the walls with erotic symbols, is either a criminal or a degenerate."[69]

But too often lost in the discussions of "Ornament and Crime" is that Loos was utilizing satire to make his point. Those in the audience in Vienna in January 1910 understood that some of his comments were intended to be funny – even while making a serious point. The Viennese Expressionist poet Albert Ehrenstein, who was a member of the circle around Kraus and Loos, wrote of one of Loos's talks a few years later: "Adolf Loos presented his serious thoughts in an extremely amusing form. The anecdotes, which he used to illustrate the lack of culture on the part of the Viennese, were like precise target shooting."[70] Loos did not mean that Hoffmann and the others using ornament were literally criminals – even if he found their actions deeply troubling. He often employed a satirical tone in his writings and impromptu talks, lapsing at times into Viennese dialect to reinforce the humor. This sort of caustic, yet entertaining, critique was a staple of the Viennese cabarets and *feuilleton* writers. Loos's close friends Kraus and Peter Altenberg were both masters of the medium, and Loos, borrowing from them, adopted the technique in his writing very early – before the turn of the century.

Still, Loos's yoking together of the continued use of ornament with crime or criminality was intended to do more than amuse the audience or inflame his opponents. His aim was to demonstrate the futility and inappropriateness of the attempts of the "artist designers" to "devise" a modern aesthetic.

The idea that ornament was linked with criminal behavior was not entirely of Loos's making. As a number of scholars have pointed out, the writings of the Italian criminologist Cesare Lombroso, in particular Lombroso's *L'uomo delinquente* (*The Criminal Man*) probably inspired Loos's fusing of ornament and the behavior of the criminal underworld.[71]

Lombroso, who had studied in Padua, Vienna, and Paris, was teaching at the University of Pavia at the time he wrote *L'uomo delinquente*. He asserted that there was a clear connection between tattoos and criminality since only criminals and primitive peoples tattooed themselves; criminals, he contended, were "atavists," or evolutionary throwbacks, who echoed in their personalities the crude instincts of primitive humanity. Tattoos, so Lombroso thought, were akin to corporeal stigmata, betraying the inner, biological nature of the criminal disposition. In *L'uomo delinquente*, which was translated into German in 1887, he writes: "Tattooing is one of the striking symptoms of humans in a raw state, in their most primitive form."[72] (In his chapter on the "biology and psychology of born criminals," he observes that nearly half of the criminals he studied bore tattoos.[73])

Loos was undoubtedly aware of Lombroso's central tenets, although there is no evidence that he actually read *L'uomo delinquente*.[74] The text fills two thick volumes, and much of it is concerned with the physical and psychological profiles of various criminal types. It is more likely that Loos became familiar with Lombroso's work second-hand, either through the newspapers or magazines, where his ideas were often referenced, or, possibly, in his discussions with Kraus. Kraus was intensely interested in issues of morality and the criminal justice system, and the problems of ethics and social behavior recur frequently in his essays in *Die Fackel*. In the years prior to 1910, he makes mention of Lombroso more than a half-dozen times, revealing extensive familiarity with his ideas.

If Loos did indeed borrow from Lombroso, he combined the Italian criminologist's theories with ideas from other sources. One of these was apparently Owen Jones. In his preface to *The Grammar of Ornament* (1856) is an engraving of the tattooed face of a Maori woman, of which Jones writes: "in this very barbarous practice the principles of the very highest ornamental art are manifest, every line upon the face is the best adapted to develop the natural features. . . . The ornament of a savage tribe, being the result of a natural instinct, is necessarily always true to its purpose."[75] Jones's description corresponds to Loos's insistence that the "compulsion to decorate one's face and anything else within reach is the origin of the fine arts. It is the childish babble of painting."[76]

It is possible, too, that Loos saw in the collections of the Naturhistorisches (Natural History) Museum in Vienna the Maori art the Austrian explorer and naturalist Andreas Reischek had collected in New Zealand in the 1870s and 1880s.[77] Over twelve years, Reischek assembled more than 450 Maori objects, including weapons, agricultural tools, canoe ornaments, house carvings, and articles of personal adornment – and images of Maori with tattoos. The museum acquired Reischek's collection and displayed it prominently.

But an even more likely source for his notion of the primitive Papuan may have been the writings of the Viennese anthropologist and ethnologist Rudolf Pöch, who undertook an expedition to New Guinea from 1901 to 1906 and, upon his return to Vienna in 1907, began to publish the results of his studies – just at the time that Loos began employing the "primitive Papuan" in his texts and lectures. Pöch's photographs of the indigenous peoples he encountered and his recordings of their languages and songs were widely discussed in the Viennese press, and they may have been the immediate source for his imagery in "Ornament and Crime."[78]

Yet central for Loos's conception of cultural development was not only the figure of the Papuan but the idea he evidently took from Lombroso that the meaning of behaviors, such as tattooing, was relative: "We have also pointed out that many actions considered criminal in civilized communities are normal and legitimate practices among primitive races. It is evident, therefore, that such actions are natural to the early stages, both of social evolution and individual psychic development."[79] Loos writes in "Ornament and Crime": "The Papuan slaughters his enemies and consumes them. He is no criminal. If, however, a modern person kills someone and eats him, he is criminal or a degenerate. The Papuan tattoos his skin, his boat, his paddle – in short, everything he can lay his hands on. He is not a criminal. The modern person who tattoos himself is either a criminal or a degenerate."[80]

Loos's understanding of the trajectory of cultural development – in particular, his equation of ornament and degeneracy – also doubtless had foundations in the writings of Max Nordau. Born into a Hungarian Jewish family in Budapest in 1849, Nordau had emerged by the end of the century as one of the preeminent political and social journalists in Europe, writing dispatches from Paris for the Vienna *Neue Freie Presse*, the Berlin *Vossische Zeitung*, and other Central European newspapers. His 1893 book *Entartung* (Degeneration), which had sounded a fierce critique of modernism, was widely read throughout Europe at the turn of the century and unleashed a fervid controversy about the nature and qualities of the new trends in literature and painting.[81] Nordau borrowed many of his themes from Lombroso – his "dear and honored master" – to whom he dedicated the work. Disillusioned by what he later called the "spirit of churlishness and brutality" of the new art, he assailed the modernists in the same terms that Lombroso applied to the wayward and the backward "atavists" he encountered in his clinical practice.[82] "Degenerates," Nordau writes in the preface to *Entartung*, "are not always criminals, prostitutes, anarchists, and pronounced lunatics; they are often authors and artists ... who satisfy their unhealthy impulses ... with the pen and pencil."[83] The best palliative against the "willfulness" of the new art, he insists, is a return to the "irresistible and unchangeable" principles of science, to the laws of causality, observation, and knowledge. Only through discursive reasoning could art regain clarity of formulation and expression. In extolling scientific progress, Nordau also enunciates his allegiance to Darwinian evolution. He was convinced that humans could not divorce themselves from the need to adapt to the changing physical world; artists who sought refuge in pure flights of imagination – "mystics" and "egomaniacs," in his words – were degenerates who impeded social and cultural progress.[84]

Loos apparently encountered Nordau's writings in the later 1890s, after his return from the United States. It is likely that it was again Kraus who inspired his interest. Kraus references Nordau repeatedly in *Die Fackel*, and the notion of degeneration surfaces often in his essays. Unlike Lombroso's books, Loos's writings suggest more than a superficial grasp of Nordau's main theses. In his essay "Kulturentartung," for example, he pairs Nordau's belief in decadence and degenerate art with a scathing critique of the German Werkbund and its aims, and the same themes reappear in "Ornament and Crime." In what seems to be a thinly veiled assault on the Symbolist painters, for example, Loos writes: "a person of our time, who smears the walls with erotic symbols out of an inner compulsion, is either a criminal or a degenerate... One can measure the cultural level of a country by the degree to which its toilet walls are covered with graffiti."[85]

Such rhetoric, at once dismissive and disparaging, could have come straight out of *Entartung*. Loos's critique also echoes Nordau's essential conservatism, especially his belief that new advances in art and culture had to be based upon previous developments. Nordau vehemently opposed the "invention" of new artistic forms; he was convinced that true cultural evolution had to be the product of "disciplined progress" that was an outcome of a "philosophy of self-restraint."[86] In "Ornament and Crime," Loos expresses this idea by drawing a comparison between the culture of the "aristocrats" of urban society – those who were thoroughly modern in outlook – with those who were less developed, and therefore less possessed of self-restraint: "I can accept the ornament of the African, the Persian, the Slovak peasant woman, my shoemaker, because they have no other means to achieve elevated states of being. We, on the other hand, possess the art that has superseded ornament. After the trials and tribulations of the day, we can go hear Beethoven or *Tristan*. My shoemaker can't do that. I can't take away his joy because I have nothing to replace it with. But anyone who goes to hear the Ninth Symphony and then sits down to design a wallpaper pattern is either a criminal or a degenerate."[87]

Loos's conception of ornamental development was also a continuation of the discourse on the subject by Gottfried Semper and Alois Riegl. In *Der Stil*, published in the early 1860s, Semper had considered the ornament problem outside the framework of Darwinian evolution, arguing that it arose organically from particular cultural matrices and that it was the product of specific material and technological conditions.[88] Riegl, writing three decades later in *Stilfragen*, rejected both Semper's assertions about the connections between structure, craft methods, and ornament and Darwin's ideas of natural selection.[89] Loos, who seems to have had a more than adequate grasp of both theorists' ideas, advanced this discussion by linking the development of ornament directly to cultural evolution. He appears to have taken over the belief in a progressive aesthetic from Nordau and, by extension, Darwin (although the latter, in his final works, rejected the idea of a purely aesthetic dimension in natural selection). "Ornament and Crime" is thus both an outcome and a contribution to the nineteenth-century discussion of evolution; it expands the discourse on social Darwinism à la Herbert Spencer (whose ideas were also no doubt known to Loos, at least in watered-down fashion) within a widened cultural framework.[90]

What is particularly arresting in “Ornament and Crime” is Loos’s attempt to link cultural evolution with a biological imperative. He seeks to establish this connection at the outset of the essay with an allusion to the so-called law of recapitulation, writing, “In the womb the human embryo passes through all the stages of development the animal kingdom has gone through.”[91]

The original statement of this idea came from the German biologist Ernst Haeckel, who famously maintained that there was a connection between “the history of the embryo (ontogeny)” and “the history of race (phylogeny).”[92] Loos was hardly alone in adapting Haeckel’s ideas; his books and essays were widely read and discussed at the time. Haeckel’s *Kunstformen der Natur* (Art Forms of Nature, 1899–1903) included vivid color illustrations of flora and fauna that inspired the stylized depictions of natural forms of a number of Jugendstil artists.[93] Loos also apparently borrowed Haeckel’s belief in an originary *Kunsttrieb*, or drive toward artistic expression inherent in all organisms, a notion that had a widespread impact on the thinking of turn-of-the-century educators and cultural reformers.[94]

Later writers reproached Loos for his somewhat cursory and loose appropriations from Lombroso, Nordau, and Haeckel. Reyner Banham, for example, writing in the late 1950s, dismissed Loos’s attempts to ground his ideas on ornament in the writings of Lombroso and the other nineteenth-century thinkers as “*Schlagobers-Philosophie* that whisks up into an exciting dish on the café table, and then collapses as you look at it, like a cooling soufflé. It is not a reasoned argument,” he continues, “but a succession of fast-spieling double-takes and non sequiturs holding together a precarious rally of clouds of witness – café-Freudianism, café-anthropology, café-criminology.”[95] But Banham and other later commentators have missed the point: Loos’s argument about the evolution of ornament may indeed be erected on a flimsy theoretical foundation, but he never attempted to posit a scholarly case; his essay was a cultural inquiry and part of a more open dialogue. He intended from the outset to entertain his audience, castigate his opponents, and establish his positions. “Ornament and Crime,” like all of Loos’s essays, was intensely personal and subjective; he sought to reach his audience through an appeal to what he thought was common sense.

Loos’s writing style in “Ornament and Crime” is also revealing. His sentences in German are stark and simply composed, their tone often familiar, even conversational. His writing betrays no pretension or concealment of thoughts behind a screen of intellectualism. He assumed that most in his audience would be at least vaguely familiar with the ideas of Lombroso, Nordau, and Haeckel.

But if the mood of "Ornament and Crime" is polemical, it is not directly prescriptive. Despite later assertions to the contrary, Loos also did not intend for his talk to be a programmatic manifesto – at least not in the usual sense. He had been producing related designs – with very little or no applied ornament – for more than a decade, and some, such as his unrealized design for a commercial and residential building for the Allgemeine Verkehrsbank on the Mariahilfer Straße in 1904, were even more insistent in their repudiation of conventional architectural decoration than the Michaelerplatz building. If the essay was later seen as a justification for Loos's design strategy, it was not a recipe for formal architectural solutions.[96] Loos never mentions the Michaelerplatz building or any of his other works in the surviving written versions of the talk, nor do the various texts contain any specific architectural references. Only later, at the end of 1910, when he began combining "Ornament and Crime" with "Architecture" in his public speeches, would he specifically address the problems associated with the building's design.

The Ornament Debate

The larger context of the talk, then, was not initially Loos's radical architecture and design but the ongoing debate about the use and appropriateness of ornament in the German-language architectural press. The period between 1907 and 1910 saw the publication of a number of articles that dealt with the problem of modern ornament.[97] The question had been stirred up in part by the ornamental excesses of the Jugendstil. But it was also an outcome of the mounting discussion in Germany and Austria about the functionalist architecture and design that was then just beginning to emerge.

The immediate trigger for the debate on ornament may have been the appearance of an essay by the German critic Joseph August Lux in *Innen-Dekoration* in 1907. Lux, who would later go on to write studies of both Joseph Maria Olbrich and Otto Wagner, asserted that the "renewal of ornament" by the reform architects and designers at the turn of the century was "the first creative accomplishment of modern art" and that it had filled applied art "with the spiritual life of the new age," which had in turn strengthened all the other arts.[98] His and similar pronouncements from other writers touched off a series of responses from critics of the Jugendstil, most of them arguing that the recourse to ornament had not been the salvation of design, but a serious misstep.

The following April, the critic Richard Schaukal published a scathing attack on those calling for the development of modern ornament. His article in *Deutsche Kunst und Dekoration*, "Gegen das Ornament" (Against Ornament), begins with a paragraph that could have come from Loos's pen: "If a thinking person today, who is vexed, even saddened, by the commercialized culture of the present, asks himself why it is that the world, at least in terms of that which is man-made, has become so very ugly and disconcerting, it will occur to him, if he has sharp eyes and a sense of the joy of beauty, what the answer is: the evil foe is ornament."[99] Schaukal, who knew Loos and his anti-ornamentalist views well, attacked ornament as "superfluous" and "purposeless." He characterized the work of the Secessionists as a symptom of the "ornamental disease" (Ornamentkrankheit) and lauded Loos as the only architect who had a clear vision of the future – one without ornament.[100]

The German critic Wilhelm Michel responded in *Innen-Dekoration* in July 1909, presenting a spirited defense of traditional architectural ornament, but agreeing with Schaukal that the Secessionists' tendency to divorce ornament from the logic of material and structure – in Michel's words, the "kulturlose Emanzipierung des Ornaments" (uncultured emancipation of ornament) – had resulted in a mounting loss of faith in ornamental design. He suggested, however, that this development might have had a positive impact: "In all likelihood, the historic verdict of the future will be that the Jugendstil did achieve something positive: at least it possessed the will to forge something creatively new. It was destructive and it generated new possibilities – though the latter was only an indirect byproduct."[101]

Another German critic, Otto Scheffers, offered a somewhat different view of the ornament problem in "Zweckform und Ornament" (Functional Form and Ornament), which appeared in *Deutsche Kunst und Dekoration* later the same year. Although not rejecting ornament entirely ("it would be just as foolish to condemn all ornament ... as it would be to apply it everywhere willy-nilly"), Scheffers asserted that the application of ornament to objects of daily use had undermined the appearance of utility and cloaked their functional form (Zweckform). Ornament, he contended, should be generally reserved for works of art: "Because ornament demands more of our eyes and our minds than smooth, even surfaces, richly applied ornament is easier to bear on objects that we see only seldom or for short periods than it is on those that we are forced to look at or use all the time."[102]

There were also some who continued to defend both ornament and the modern arts and crafts. The Berlin architect and designer Anton Jaumann asked in an article in *Innen-Dekoration* in January 1910, "is the debate is really over?"

Jaumann criticized the whole constellation of modernist aesthetics – in his words, "functionality, simplicity, constructivism, and material honesty" – suggesting that such approaches had only "relative value."[103] The German art historian and critic Otto Schulze-Elberfeld introduced an alternative defense of ornament in 1910. He conceded that it had been misused and was losing its power in the modern age, but he reminded his readers that ornament still had a communicative role to play – "Genuine ornament is like a language" – and that role was still important.[104] The problem, as Schulze-Elberfeld saw it, was that few working architects or designers were still fluent in the authentic vernacular of ornament, and this would ultimately doom "ornamental symbolism."

Loos was aware of this discussion; without doubt, he regarded "Ornament and Crime" as a contribution to – indeed, an advancement of – the debate. He may have been the most voluble of those assailing the continued reliance on ornament, but he was far from alone. Nor was Loos's a solitary voice calling for the removal of art from the design of utilitarian objects. The German sociologist Georg Simmel had called for the separation of art from objects of daily use already in 1908: The products of the arts and crafts, Simmel wrote, "are intended to be integrated in daily life. For that reason, they represent the complete opposites of works of art, which belong to a world of their own."[105]

What distinguished Loos's position were two fundamental ideas: that ornament would gradually disappear on its own as part of a logical evolution of culture; and that to continue to make ornament was not only an impediment to modern progress but a contribution to the exploitation of craftspeople, who were being inadequately compensated. The latter notion grew out of Loos's understanding of the plight of traditional artisans, who were increasingly forced to compete with factory-made goods, and his strong sympathies for the Austrian Socialist movement.[106]

In a related argument, Hermann Muthesius, one of the leaders of the German Werkbund, had sounded a cautionary call against the use of machine-made ornament.

> Precisely because ... the machine has allowed us to make ornament on a mass basis, we have seen a proliferation of shoddy ornament throughout the applied arts, which has resulted in the sinking of artistic standards to deplorable depths. ... The ornamental motifs thrust into the marketplace by the millions have led to a devaluation. Ornament has become commonplace. And

> for people with taste, the development of the arts and crafts industry over the past decade has led to an accumulation of so much distaste that the phenomenon is no longer bearable.[107]

Others within the Werkbund were soon echoing Muthesius's contention that the proliferation of ornament had resulted in a decline in the standards of the applied arts, and some began to regard ornamented factory products as inferior to those with no applied decoration.[108]

Loos, however, does not consider the problem of ornament in industrial design. Nowhere in "Ornament and Crime" does he engage directly the question of mass production. His few comments that bear upon the issue have to do with the "waste" and "abuse" of materials and planned obsolescence.[109] Loos, perhaps drawing from Thorstein Veblen (or, at least, some version of his ideas), rejects the contention that modern design's rapid fall from fashion is healthy for the economy, but the meaning of the ornament problem for industry remains for him linked to his argument about the pace of cultural development. He has little to say otherwise about what the new design might mean for machine manufacturing.

Loos's beliefs were still rooted in a nineteenth-century vision of craft production. His upbringing as the son of a stonemason undoubtedly colored his ideas, but his position was also a result of the prevailing conditions in Vienna. In contrast to many other cities in Central Europe which were then developing into centers of industrial production, Vienna's economy was still focused on handicraft. Throughout Germany, the swift advance of mass production was destroying the traditional crafts. But in Vienna, which had long been a hub for "artistic production," handicraft hung onto life. The survival of many consummate artists was one of the chief reasons for the success of the Wiener Werkstätte, which relied on the very highest standards of manual fabrication. Loos's silence on industrially produced objects placed him outside the discussion then taking place within the Werkbund, even while his views would ultimately have a significant impact on the development of the new design and its applications.

The Second Berlin Talk

On March 3, 1910, Loos presented "Ornament and Crime" again, this time in Berlin. The lecture, which was sponsored by the Verein für Kunst, took place once more in the Salon Cassirer on the Viktoriastraße. Walden made all of the arrangements. He intended in part for the talk to publicize the launch of his new cultural journal *Der Sturm*. In the weeks beforehand, both Kraus and Loos worked assiduously to find subscribers in Vienna and to secure the payments, which they sent to Walden so he could cover the printing costs.[110] Loos also sent Walden a hundred crowns to advertise the lecture.[111]

The first issue of *Der Sturm*, which appeared the same day as Loos's talk, included one of his essays, "Vom armen reichen Mann" (The Poor Rich Man), as well as an advertisement for the lecture. The newspapers, however, took little notice. The *Berliner Tageblatt* ran a short announcement the day of the lecture, but the event otherwise was mostly ignored in the mainstream press.[112] Only two reviews appeared, one of them an unsigned write-up in the *Berliner Tageblatt* that was published the following day. The piece accurately outlined Loos's main arguments, paraphrasing his contention that those in modern society who continue to use ornament are either "swindlers or degenerates" (Hochstapler oder Degenerierte) and outlining his basic economic objections to ornament.[113] The extensive summary suggests that the version of the talk Loos read in Berlin was identical or very similar to his first Vienna presentation, although it is impossible to establish this for certain.

Advertisement for Loos's second Berlin presentation of "Ornament and Crime" published in *Der Sturm*, March 3, 1910, p. 8.

Three lines in the review stand out. In the first, the author incorrectly cites Loos as saying that "Ornament is crime," an assertion that would be repeated often in later years. (Loos never states in the published text that ornament *is* crime, but, rather, that a "modern person" who uses it "is a criminal or degenerate.")[114] The reviewer also encapsulates the meaning of Loos's lecture for the applied arts: "Loos has now demonstrated that the entire history of the applied arts itself represents an adornment" – implying that the new ornamental movement in design contradicted the inner truth of modernism – exactly Loos's contention. It is notable, though, that the reviewer makes no mention of the possible impact of Loos's ideas on architecture; he or she understood that the lecture involved the design of objects of daily use – again, as Loos intended. The reviewer's important third statement reveals that Loos once more received a favorable audience response, but that the event was sparsely attended: "The twenty people in the audience yesterday gave him a warm round of applause."[115]

A second review, which appeared a week and a half later in the Berlin satirical magazine *Der Ulk*, a supplement to the *Berliner Tageblatt*, was much less positive. The unsigned piece made light of Loos's ideas, painting him as a fanatic who wanted to have "fifty of Berlin's most prominent citizens" – its leading industrialists and pattern makers – tortured and then jailed for their alleged criminal application of ornament. "Away with murderous ornament!," Loos is quoted as screaming to the reporter, while trying to stab him with a dripping paintbrush. The reporter concluded drolly: "The next time I will encounter him more carefully, in a completely unornamented tuxedo."[116] Loos, however, failed to find any humor in the *Ulk* review. In the April 7, 1910 edition of *Der Sturm*, he published a short, one-line rebuttal: "Dear Ulk: And I tell you, there will come a day when incarceration in a jail cell decorated by court wallpaperer [Eduard] Schulz or Professor Van de Velde will be considered a more severe sentence."[117]

Despite the reactions to his talk in the *Berliner Tageblatt* and *Der Ulk*, Loos must have been disappointed. Some years later, in an autobiographical sketch, he sought to put a different face on the events. Writing in the third person, he describes the impact of the lectures: "Aside from his work [on the Goldman & Salatsch Building], he undertook lecture tours in Austria and Germany, winning with his lecture, 'Ornament and Crime' ... a large circle of supporters."[118] In fact, up to the middle of 1910, Loos's impact in both countries was still negligible, although that would change dramatically with the developing controversy about the Goldman & Salatsch Building later in the year.

Shortly after the second Berlin talk, Loos left Vienna, traveling south to search for sources for marble for the Goldman & Salatsch Building. He went first to Morocco and Algeria, then to Greece and Italy. By May or early June, he had returned to the city.[119] For most of the remainder of the summer, he worked on the drawings for the Steiner House and the façades for the Goldman & Salatsch Building, which was already under construction. By mid-September, the building had been plastered, and it was then that the newspapers began to report on Loos's intentions to leave the upper stories of the façade unornamented. Almost immediately, the municipal authorities suspended the building permit; by the end of the month a vociferous public controversy had erupted.

Loos defended himself in several newspaper articles, but his explanations of his intentions for the design did little to stem the growing outcry.[120] In late November, one of the city council members, Karl Rykl, attacked Loos's building, calling it "a monstrosity" ("ein Scheusal") and demanding a redesign of the façades.[121]

It was in this context that Loos presented his lecture "Über Architektur" in Berlin in early December 1910. Loos spoke this time in the much larger Hagensaal, on the Wilhelmstraße. The sponsor for the talk once more was Walden's Verein für Kunst, but the idea for the event appears to have come from Loos, who evidently hoped that a positive reception for his ideas in Berlin might help to deflect some of the criticism in Vienna.[122]

VEREIN FÜR KUNST
Donnerstag, den 8. Dezember, abends 8 Uhr
Architektenhaus (Hagensaal) Wilhelmstr. 92/93
ADOLF LOOS
Vortrag: ÜBER ARCHITEKTUR.
Karten à Mk. 3 u. 2 an der Abendkasse.

Advertisement for Loos's presentation of "Über Architektur" in Berlin, from *Der Sturm*, December 8, 1910, p. 300.

The lecture, a portion of which was printed in *Der Sturm* a week later, engaged the problems of modern architecture, although the version later published in *Trotzdem* contains only a single explicit reference to the Michaelerplatz building.[123] Much of it was a restatement of "Ornament and Crime." Indeed, several phrases reappear exactly, including Loos's contention that the "evolution of culture is synonymous with the removal of ornament from objects of daily use."[124] His references to the primitive Papuan also recur, as do his remarks about tattoos as symbols of degeneration and stylistic obsolescence.[125] The text repeats, too, Loos's barbs at applied art and his defense of artisanal production. "Architecture," however, presents a greatly expanded version of Loos's cultural argument, applying his critique to building in the modern age. At its core is Loos's attempt to draw the distinction between art – monumental architecture – and ordinary building – the vernacular forms and approaches of traditional builders. His main argument is simple and direct: forthright and legible designs that communicate their meaning clearly are the only legitimate building form: "A living room should be comfortable, a house appear livable. A courthouse must look threatening to those contemplating crime. A bank must say: here your money is being held in safe-keeping by honest people. ... If we come across a mound in the woods that is six feet long and three feet wide, we become somber and recognize: someone is buried here. *That is architecture.*"[126] At the end of the piece, Loos adds to this argument: the culture of the West, he writes, is founded upon "the recognition of the transcendent greatness of classical antiquity." The Secessionists and other modernists, like the historicists before them, had forgotten the abiding lessons of classicism and strayed from the path of true architecture.[127]

In combining his original arguments about the "cultural problem" of ornament in the applied arts with his principles of building in a manner that was consistent with vernacular traditions and classical precepts, Loos's "Architecture" broadly restated the principal tenets of "Ornament and Crime." Over the next year, the two essays would become closely linked as Loos sought to win the battle over the Michaelerplatz building.

The Munich and Prague Lectures and Their Aftermath

A little more than a week after giving "Über Architektur" in Berlin, Loos presented "Ornament and Crime" in Munich. The talk took place on December 17 in the grand ballroom of the Hotel Vier Jahreszeiten on the Maximilliansstraße.[128] The sponsor was the Neuer Verein, a group of mostly younger artists, writers, and designers analogous to the Vienna Akademischer Verband für Literatur und Musik. In contrast to the polite, even tepid, reaction to his talks in Vienna and Berlin, the response in Munich, at least during the discussion after Loos had finished speaking, became heated. Loos, an anonymous reporter wrote in the *Munchner Neueste Nachrichten* the following day, had "declared war on ornament." For him, "it is a has-been, dead, a vestige of a long-dead culture ..." Although much of the audience was "fascinated by Loos's presentation" and charmed by his "amusing defense" of his ideas, the three audience members who spoke afterward, including the painter, illustrator, and designer Fritz Erler, one of the mainstays of the journal *Simplicissimus*, had all "assailed Loos's statements."[129] The response was hardly surprising. Munich had been the leading center of the Jugendstil in Germany around the turn of the century, and in 1910 it was still a hotbed for the new ornamental design. Loos expected that he would meet with some opposition to his views there, though the vocal outcry apparently surprised even him.

Loos found no time, however, to mount a response. He returned to Vienna for the Christmas holidays, and, a few weeks later, he and Bessie, whose health was worsening, departed for Libya. Loos left her at a sanatorium in the desert oasis town of Biskra and returned to Vienna.

In mid-March, he repeated "Ornament and Crime" again, this time in Prague. The Polytechnischer Verein, a student organization at the German Technical University, which housed one of the three architecture schools in the city, sponsored the lecture. Unlike his second Berlin and Munich lectures, the Prague talk was well publicized. On the day of the presentation, the *Prager Tagblatt* profiled Loos in a feature article, calling him "one of the most interesting figures" among Viennese architects and a representative of the "radicalism of functionalism," a principle he "demonstrated in his new building on the Michaelerplatz."[130] Loos spoke in German, but it is likely that a number of the younger Czech-speaking architects attended, as did the writer Franz Kafka.[131]

The next day, a review of the lecture in the *Prager Tagblatt* (probably written by critic Ludwig Steiner) offered a very positive assessment. The first third of the article summarized the basic points from what was now Loos's standard text for "Ornament and Crime." The author refers to Loos's argument that "a person of the year 1911 can no longer apply ornament," confirming that Loos continued to change the internal dating in the piece to keep it contemporary. What is most noteworthy in the review, however, is the middle portion, which recapitulates the main ideas in "Über Architektur," including Loos's opening image of a simple farmhouse in the landscape. The reviewer notes that Loos subsequently spoke about his "building on the Michaelerplatz," which was now nearing completion.[132]

The review reveals that Loos had begun to combine "Ornament and Crime" with portions of "Über Architektur." Merging these texts would become his standard strategy over the next year and half, as he quoted from "Ornament and Crime" in defending his radical design. Indeed, "Ornament and Crime" now became Loos's stump speech, which he used in a number of variations to justify his work and enlist allies. This is why so many of those who later recalled hearing the lecture associated it with the controversy over the Michaelerplatz commission.

The Prague audience, at least to judge from the *Prager Tagblatt* review, was far from hostile. At the end, the author writes that Loos's talk "captivated the listeners, which mostly included architectural professionals, to such a degree that although many had strong private reservations, there was thunderous applause afterward."[133] The audience's friendly response is all the more striking when one considers that Prague in 1911 was already in the throes of Czech Cubism, and some of the younger Czech-speaking architects were highly critical of the call for *Sachlichkeit* and functionality in architecture and design.[134]

The following day, Loos presented another lecture, "Vom Stehen, Gehen, Sitzen, Schlafen, Essen und Trinken" (On Standing, Walking, Sitting, Sleeping, Eating, and Drinking), at the Vienna Technische Hochschule, in the lecture hall of the Elektrotechnisches Institut.[135] The essay, excerpts of which were reprinted in *Der Sturm* in November 1911, is among the least known of Loos's texts from this period.[136] It draws on many of the themes from "Ornament and Crime," in particular Loos's assault on applied art and his affirmation of the value of traditional craft. Missing, however, are the vivid images from "Ornament and Crime": the primitive Papuan, tattoos, the references to criminality. Loos substituted a straightforward argument about the ways in which objects of daily use should serve their basic functions. In its celebration of folk and everyday models, the text echoes his reasoning in "Über Architektur." The published version in *Der Sturm* makes no direct reference to the Goldman & Salatsch Building, but, in November 1911, Loos did so explicitly when he gave an expanded version of the lecture in Berlin on Walden's invitation to come and speak about his building.[137]

Throughout the summer and fall of 1911, Loos continued to fend off calls to redesign the upper façades of the Michaelerplatz building. But by early summer, weakened from the stress of the controversy, he began suffering from

Adolf Loos, Goldman & Salatsch Building, Vienna, late 1911, with the five window boxes installed. Bildarchiv Foto Marburg, Philipps-Universität.

a serious bout of gastric ulcers. He spent much of next several months at a sanatorium near Vienna and, later, a pension in the mountains, slowly recovering.

In September, Loos, still not fully healthy, launched once more his defense of the building. To deflect the controversy, he drew up a proposal to add bronze window boxes to its upper stories. In October, without securing a building permit, he had five boxes fabricated and mounted on the façade to test the effect. The city building authorities ordered that the boxes be removed, but Loos and the clients refused to comply. In mid-December, Loos delivered yet another lecture, "Mein Haus am Michaelerplatz," once more championing his design. The talk's sponsor was the Akademischer Verband für Literatur und Musik, and Loos spoke this time in the large Sophiensaal to more than 2,500.[138] "Mein Haus am Michaelerplatz" was a triumph for Loos, who managed to win over most of the audience. The newspapers, which had been generally critical up to this time, also reported favorably on the lecture, and a number of them applauded Loos's proposed compromise of adding the window boxes.[139] On March 29, 1912, the city council officially sanctioned the design, and two months later the decision was made final.[140]

Despite his triumph, Loos continued to present "Ornament and Crime" for another year, delivering the talk at least once more in Vienna in 1912 and again in 1913.[141] During the controversy, or possibly in the period just afterward, he also presented the talk again in Munich, although the exact date is unknown.[142] The last documented presentation of "Ornament and Crime" took place in Copenhagen on April 5, 1913.[143]

Poster for Adolf Loos's 1913 presentation of "Ornament and Crime" in Vienna. Wien Museum, Vienna.

ORNEMENT ET CRIME

On sait que l'embryon humain passe dans le sein de la mère par toutes les phases de l'évolution du règne animal. L'homme, à sa naissance, reçoit du monde extérieur les mêmes impressions qu'un petit chien. Son enfance résume les étapes de l'histoire humaine : à deux ans, il a les sens et l'intelligence d'un Papou ; à quatre ans, d'un ancien Germain. A six ans, il voit le monde par les yeux de Socrate, à huit ans par ceux de Voltaire. C'est à huit ans qu'il prend conscience du violet, la couleur que le XVIIIe siècle a découverte. Car avant cette date les violettes étaient bleues et la pourpre rouge. Et nos physiciens montrent aujourd'hui dans le spectre solaire des couleurs qui déjà ont un nom, mais dont la connaissance est réservée aux générations à venir.

Le petit enfant et le Papou vivent en deça de toute morale. Le Papou tue ses ennemis et les mange : il n'est pas un criminel. Mais un homme moderne qui tue son voisin et le mange ne peut-être qu'un criminel ou un dégénéré. Le Papou tatoue sa peau, sa pirogue, sa pagaie, tout ce qui lui tombe sous la main. Il n'est pas un criminel. Un homme moderne qui se tatoue est un criminel ou un dégénéré. Dans beaucoup de prisons, la proportion des tatoués s'élève à 80 °/₀. Les tatoués qui vivent en liberté sont des criminels latents ou des aristocrates dégénérés. Il arrive que leur vie semble irréprochable jusqu'au bout. C'est qu'ils sont morts avant leur crime.

247

First page of the French translation of "Ornament and Crime," translated by Marcel Ray. From *Les cahiers d'aujourd'hui* 5 (June 1913), p. 247.

One of the most persistent myths about "Ornament and Crime" has to do with the date and location of its first publication. A number of scholars have written that Loos first published the piece in 1908 (relying on the incorrect dating in *Trotzdem* and other sources), or in 1910. In fact, the essay was not published until 1913, in French, in the June issue of *Les cahiers d'aujourd'hui*.[144]

The translator was Marcel Ray, a professor at the University of Montpellier, who was one of the leading Germanists in France. The little surviving evidence suggests that Ray may have met Loos through the educational reformer Eugenie Schwarzwald, who was a member of the large circle around Kraus, Loos, and Altenberg.[145] It is unclear when the two men became acquainted, but Ray published a translation of a large portion of "Über Architektur" under the title "L'Architecture et le style moderne" in the December 1912 issue of *Les cahiers d'aujourd'hui*.[146] The following spring or early summer, he translated the text of "Ornament and Crime" for the journal. Many years later, Reyner Banham, in *Theory and Design in the First Machine Age*, reported erroneously that the translation had come from the journal's editor, Georges Besson, and that it was "lively, but somewhat bowdlerized, and fairly heavily cut."[147] In fact, Ray's translation is generally faithful to the original, and in at least one place actually improves upon it. The key line, "evolution der kultur ist gleichbedeutend mit dem entfernen des ornamentes aus dem gebrauchsgegenstande," Ray translates as "A mesure que la culture développe, l'ornement disparaît des objets usuels," substituting "disparaît" (disappears) for "entfernen" (removal), a change that rather better conveys Loos's conviction that ornament would gradually vanish on its own.[148] Banham is correct, though, when he asserts that the publication of "Ornament and Crime" in *Les cahiers d'aujourd'hui* made the essay accessible to a large international audience.[149] The text would have a pronounced impact on the avant-garde in France, including Le Corbusier, who republished it in *L'Esprit nouveau* in 1920.[150] Excerpts of the essay were reprinted again, in 1926, in *L'Architecture vivante*. The first German-language publication did not come until 1929, when Kulka (and apparently also Glück) prepared it for publication in the *Frankfurter Zeitung*[151] The essay was reprinted two weeks later, in the *Prager Tagblatt*, but it was its appearance in *Trotzdem* a little more than a year later that would become the standard source for the text until the publication of Loos's complete essays in the early 1960s.[152]

The foreword that introduced "Ornament and Crime" when it was published in the *Prager Tagblatt* contributed greatly to the subsequent myths about the essay. Kulka evidently wrote the text, but he undoubtedly did so with Loos's input. It seems to convey how Loos wanted "Ornament and Crime" to be remembered, although many of the assertions distort the historical record.

> This article by the Viennese architect, written in 1908, at which time it was the cause of riots among the applied artists in Munich, but received with rapturous applause when delivered as a lecture in Berlin, has never before been published in German ... It demonstrates to us today that, at a time when *art nouveau* was flourishing, Adolf Loos was perhaps the only person who was clear about what is *modern*. Just as the buildings Adolf Loos designed twenty years ago, and which at the time aroused a storm of indignation, are now accepted as expressions of pure functional form.[153]

It is unclear why Loos thought it was necessary to alter the story. It is certainly possible that he could no longer recall some of the details, although several changes, which paint him as an original thinker and heroic martyr for the cause of modernism, appear deliberate. The reinvention of history may have been a reaction on Loos's part to his gradual disappearance from the front ranks of the modernists during the 1920s – even though he was still widely recognized at the time for his anti-ornament crusade, even among the younger generation of the avant-garde.

His recasting of the story of "Ornament and Crime" is all the more intriguing because in the mid-1920s Loos had taken efforts to correct some of the misunderstandings about his attack on ornament. In "Ornament und Erziehung" (Ornament and Education), which originally appeared in the Czech-language architectural journal *Náš směr* (Our Direction) and was reprinted in *Trotzdem*, Loos rebutted the notion that he had called for the eradication of all ornament: "ornament will disappear on its own ... as part of a natural process"; but there were, he explained, design applications for which ornament might be proper and relevant.[154]

The extent of Loos's role in the reshaping of the story of "Ornament and Crime" will probably remain unknown. What is indisputable is that after 1929 the accounts of the appearance of the essay diverge from the known facts. When

"Ornament and Crime" was finally published in German in 1929, most read it in isolation, without knowing Loos's experiences in the period around 1909–12. Ultimately, however, it is the integration of the essay into Loos's campaign against the applied artists, beginning in early 1910, and the place it occupied in his later defense of the Goldman & Salatsch Building, that explain its origins and the evolution of its meaning.

Ornament and Meaning

What makes "Ornament and Crime" a singular document among Loos's texts rests not with its originality. There was, in fact, little in the essay that was entirely new for him. He had developed most of the substance of his arguments in the decade before he finally recorded it – in late 1909 and early 1910 – and other theorists and critics had already anticipated many of his ideas in the preceding years. The essay's novelty lies instead in Loos's assemblage of his arguments in a complete form – as a fully developed polemic.

But Loos did more than to bring his ideas together: he sharpened his critique, wielding images and satire to provoke reactions from his opponents. "Ornament and Crime" was a radicalization of Loos's assault on ornament: it attempted to settle scores – with Hoffmann and the other Viennese Secessionists, in particular – and speak the final word in the broader ornament debate.

The essay marked a shift in direction for Loos. It corresponded with his move away from a practice focused on interior design to the design of architecture. He wrote it at the moment when he was laboring on his first building. Although it does not engage the question of the new architecture directly, it imagines an aesthetic liberated from ornament. What Loos believed to be his great discovery – that the trajectory of cultural evolution was leading away from the use of ornament for utilitarian objects – was a historical overview. "Ornament and Crime" was at once a critique of the recent past and a glance into the modernist future.

What has often been misunderstood is that Loos did not lose his faith in ornament, but rather in our capacity to make and use new ornament. The crime was not ornament, but the fact that so many failed to acknowledge the unavoidable truth: that ornament was losing its relevance in modern architecture and design. Loos's unwillingness to exclude the possible application of ornament in monumental architecture – a notion he articulates lucidly in "Architecture" –

stems from his deep faith in tradition. But he also believed that ornament was dying and could not be revived. The stridency of "Ornament and Crime" grew out of his irritation with those who disregarded this reality.

In the end, Loos's famed polemic was more than a refutation of modern ornament. The circumstances surrounding his writing of the essay and his presentations of it in the years from 1909 to 1913 offer a record of the unfolding of his aesthetic concerns and preoccupations at a pivotal moment. What had begun as an effort to provoke his opponents and restate his intentions for his own work became, in the course of the controversy surrounding the Goldman & Salatsch Building, a defense of himself and his design. "Ornament and Crime" was a declaration of Loos's beliefs, a reflection of his conclusions about the essential character of the new age, a diatribe directed at his opponents, a weapon in the battle over his Michaelerplatz design, and a summary of his travails and triumphs.

3 | Loos and the Biedermeier Revival in Vienna

In 1903, in the second – and, as it turned out, final – issue of his short-lived magazine, *Das Andere: Ein Blatt zur Einführung abendländischer Kultur in Österreich* (The Other: A Periodical for the Introduction of Western Culture to Austria), Adolf Loos published a photograph of the façade of an old storefront on Wildpretmarkt in Vienna's inner city. The establishment, he explained in an accompanying text, belonged to a family named Exinger. They had opened a butcher shop for wild game there in the 1810s, and for more than ninety years they had left the façade intact, only repainting it from time to time with its original green and white color scheme. Loos lamented that the building in which the shop was housed was slated for demolition in a few weeks' time. (The land on which it rested would become a part of the site of Jože Plečnik's new Zacherlhaus, which was completed the following year.) He insisted that, given its significance, the proper thing to do would be to save the storefront and place it in the city's museum.[1]

Loos founded his argument not on the façade's historic value or its remarkably pristine condition, but on what he thought was its usefulness as a model for modern design. In the simple, elegant lines of its façade, its vestigial classicism, and its forthright expression of middle-class values, he found an alternative to Art Nouveau and late nineteenth-century historicism.

Façade of Johann Exinger shop, Vienna, early nineteenth century (photograph ca. 1903). From Adolf Loos, *Das Andere: Ein Blatt zur Einführung abendländischer Kultur in Österreich* 1, no. 2, October 15, 1903, p. 2.

Das Andere: Ein Blatt zur Einführung abendländischer Kultur in Österreich 1, no. 2, October 15, 1903, cover.

Loos was hardly alone in turning to the aesthetic of the Biedermeier era as a source for new aesthetic ideas: many of the preeminent architects and designers in Central Europe after 1900 – Peter Behrens, Josef Hoffmann, Bruno Paul, Heinrich Tessenow, and Ludwig Mies van der Rohe – saw in the age of the Biedermeier the glimmers of an emergent and novel language for modern design and architecture. They, like Loos, regarded the revival styles of the second half of the nineteenth century as an aberration, a break from history and tradition. In turning to the first half of the century for inspiration, they sought to reestablish a connection with what they believed was an earlier, authentic past.[2]

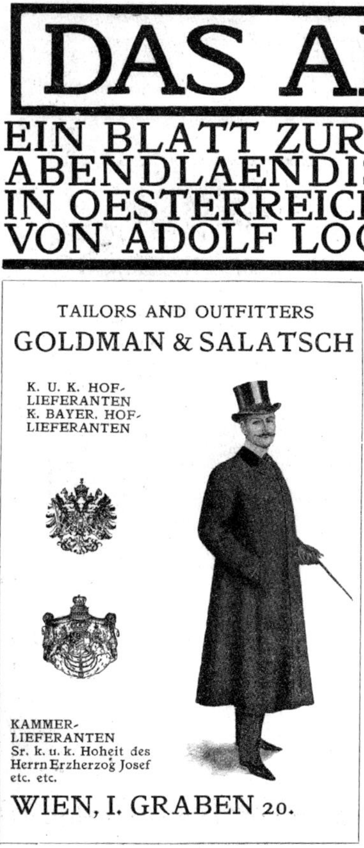

Nr. 2 WIEN, 15. OKTOBER 1903 Preis 20 h

DAS ANDERE

EIN BLATT ZUR EINFUEHRUNG ABENDLAENDISCHER KULTUR IN OESTERREICH: GESCHRIEBEN VON ADOLF LOOS I. JAHR

TAILORS AND OUTFITTERS
GOLDMAN & SALATSCH

K. U. K. HOF-LIEFERANTEN
K. BAYER. HOF-LIEFERANTEN

KAMMER-LIEFERANTEN
Sr. k. u. k. Hoheit des Herrn Erzherzog Josef etc. etc.

WIEN, I. GRABEN 20.

Société Franco-Autrichienne
pour les arts industriels

MÖBELSTOFFE

LYONER SEIDEN- UND SAMT-BROKATE

ECHTE UND IMITIERTE GOBELINS

ENGLISCHE UND FRANZÖSISCHE TEPPICHE

STICKEREIEN UND APPLIKATIONEN

SPITZENVORHÄNGE

WIEN, I. Kärntnerstrasse 55, 1. Stock

Société Franco-Autrichienne

But Loos, more perhaps than any of his contemporaries, had a particularly strong attraction to the possibilities of adapting the Biedermeier form-language. Over the course of the decade and a half between the turn of the century and the eruption of World War I, he undertook a sustained investigation of the guiding ideas of Biedermeier design. As a consequence, many of his works – whether individual furnishings, interiors, or architectural projects – betray evidence of his preoccupation with the Biedermeier aesthetic. Yet they do so in divergent and composite ways. In seeking to recast the traces of the modern style from the era "around 1800," Loos engaged a full array of strategies – at times replicating past models, at times appropriating them, at times probing their underlying meanings as a tactic to transform them. In a sense, Loos's encounter with Biedermeier amounted to an extension of late historicism, purified of the immoderation of nineteenth-century taste. His search for the essence of the new in the culture of premodern Vienna would lead him to devise a distinctive and original definition of the modern aesthetic.

The renewed interest in the Biedermeier in Viennese art and design circles began around the turn of the century.[3] It was prompted in part by a display of Biedermeier furniture in the 1901 "Winter Exhibition," held at the Österreichisches Museum für Kunst und Industrie (Austrian Museum of Art and Industry). The pieces were all replicas from the living room of a marvelously preserved early nineteenth-century country house in Atzgersdorf, then still a small village on the city's outskirts. The simplicity and directness of the ensemble struck critic Ludwig Hevesi as "enchanting," an avowal of different era, he wrote, "before factory-made furniture came in supposed Gothic or pretend Renaissance."[4] Hevesi commented that he thought it would be "foolish" to readopt the Biedermeier style; it was now "dead." Still, he suggested, its principles – "functionality, genuineness of its materials, appropriateness to its time, and the highest-quality handicraft one could imagine" (zweckecht, stoffecht, zeitecht und dazu das denkbar tüchtigste Handwerk) – remained vital.[5]

Hevesi's remarks were a reversal of what had long been the standard view of Biedermeier design: artists and architects in the second half of the nineteenth century had often derided the middle-class style of the *Vormärz* (literally, "before March," referring to the period before the revolution of 1848) as a manifestation of bourgeois unimaginativeness. For the young Viennese modernists who came on the scene around the fin de siècle, though, the unadorned façades of Biedermeier buildings and the austere forms of its furniture appeared to have inaugurated a modern tradition, one they sought to reclaim. Hevesi noted that the spirit of this Biedermeier revival seemed to be alive not only in the works of Hoffmann and his followers, but in a number of designs "à la Loos."[6]

Loos's own conversion to the possibilities of a reimagined Biedermeier form language had come a short time before. In the series of articles he published in the *Neue Freie Presse* in 1898 on the occasion of the emperor's Jubilee Exhibition, he had assailed the Secessionsstil as contrived and inauthentic. The Secessionsstil – the specific Viennese rendering of the Jugendstil – was an expression, Loos believed, of artists who had lost their moorings and were no longer aware of what constituted a true contemporary style. In its place, he proposed a return to the traditional crafts and the values of premodern Vienna. Loos's mounting allegiance to Biedermeier also derived from the belief – one he shared with many of his contemporaries – that the *Vormärz* was the last time in which a harmonious, genuine, and original culture had existed in Central Europe. The time of Beethoven, Goethe, and Schubert – a period of intellectual and artistic promise and fulfillment, of cultural accord and probity – stood for them in direct opposition to the falsity and sham pretensions of the 1880s and 1890s. Implicit within this critique, too, was a social message: Biedermeier was the aesthetic creation of the ascendant bourgeoisie, whose embrace of simplicity, hard work, and truthfulness was reflected in their surroundings and objects of daily use. The lifestyle of "around 1800" thus posed an aesthetic and moral standard, a guide to reestablishing a culture of integrity and immediacy.

The idea of Biedermeier as a *Bildungsideal* – a didactic model for young architects and designers – was given full voice in Joseph August Lux's article "Biedermeier als Erzieher" (Biedermeier as Educator), which appeared in the Viennese cultural magazine *Hohe Warte* in 1904. Lux, a prominent critic and author whose writings included biographies of Otto Wagner and Joseph Maria Olbrich, extolled the possibilities of the *Vormärz* for providing the "prerequisites for a rooted formal culture."[7] His title – indeed, his tone and mission – drew from conservative art historian Julius Langbehn's widely read book *Rembrandt als Erzieher* (1890), which had made a stirring plea for the recovery of a pan-Germanic aesthetic culture.[8] In calling for a revived sense of *Deutschtum* (Germanness), Langbehn had spurned borrowings from foreign sources, including the forms of Greco-Roman antiquity. But Lux was concerned primarily with the specific lessons Biedermeier might provide for a new domestic style. He dismissed Langbehn's anticlassicism, finding in the specific elements of Biedermeier furniture and buildings the foundations for a new style.[9]

For Lux, foremost among these was the message of *Sachlichkeit* – clarity and directness in expression – and the possibility of developing a new stylistic language based on local sources, rather than importing such ideas from England, France, or elsewhere. Lux also located other qualities in the furniture and interiors of the *Vormärz*. One of these was the notion of "liberated furniture." Tables and chairs, he suggested, might be conceived of as fully independent, and furniture could be placed freely about rooms, without engaging the surrounding architectural frame. In accord with Biedermeier precedents, he argued that furniture should be light and mobile and that it should also be comfortable. Perhaps the most salient lesson for Lux, though, had to do with functionality. He quotes the Hamburg art historian and museum director Alfred Lichtwark: "As is the case for the entire house, furniture should be raised to the highest level of practical usefulness. Only on this basis can we achieve beauty."[10]

The close pairing of functionality and beauty was already gaining currency in avant-garde circles by the first years of the new century. The suggestion that such ideas had existed previously – that, in essence, Biedermeier had presented an incipient and fecund modernism – proved to be an alluring vision for many designers and architects. Not only did it afford a strategy for a potent aesthetic vision, but it suggested that modernism might be part of a longer, evolutionary path. The new design thus might not entail a radical break with the past. For Loos, who harbored an abiding devotion to the tradition of Western classicism, the possibility of finding a route to the present without abandoning history (or classicism in the broadest sense) seemed especially welcome.[11]

Lux's article, which spelled out in great detail how the tenets of the Biedermeier aesthetic might be applied to modern design problems, was but one of a number of articles and books that propelled the renewed interest in the culture of the *Vormärz*. A year before, the Viennese art historian Joseph Folnesics had published a large illustrated folio of images of Austrian furniture and interiors from the period, *Innenräume und Hausrat der Empire- und Biedermeierzeit in Österreich-Ungarn* (Interiors and Furnishings of the Empire and Biedermeier Era in Austria-Hungary); several other prominent authors in Austria and Germany produced texts examining the Biedermeier or its revival, among them Viennese art historian Alois Riegl.[12] Lux also published a picture book on Biedermeier, *Empire und Biedermeier: Eine Sammlung von Möbeln und Innenräumen* (Empire and Biedermeier: A Collection of Furniture and Interiors), in 1906.[13] The most influential of the works propagating the idea of a revival of early nineteenth-century design, though, was Paul Mebes's two-volume folio *Um 1800:*

Architektur und Handwerk im letzten Jahrhundert ihrer traditionellen Entwicklung (Around 1800: Architecture and Crafts in the Last Century of Their Traditional Development).[14]

Mebes was a practicing architect in Berlin. He restated Lux's contention that the most meaningful lesson to be drawn from the architecture and design of the era of the neoclassical revival and Biedermeier was a return to "simplicity and modesty." He believed such a move would end forever "the wretched and shoddy works of unscrupulous mass production and uneducated speculative building" (die kläglichen Pfuschereien einer gewissenlosen Massenfabrikation und eines ungebildeten Bauspekulantentums).[15] He also reiterated Lux's ambition of retrieving the basis for a unified culture. Mebes, however, rejected the prevailing faith in the intellectualization of art and architecture. "Artists and craftsmen," he insisted, once freed from the constraints of theoreticians and the will to a new style, would come again "to speak directly to the people, through their works alone."[16] A modern aesthetic would arise directly out the ferment of everyday culture as an anonymous product of larger cultural and social forces.

Mebes's advocacy of Biedermeier was anchored in his belief that historicism and the Art Nouveau relied upon a self-conscious, willful imposition of style. His stress on the agency of a shared aesthetic over individual invention is central to his argument, and it extends as a leitmotif through the two volumes of *Um 1800*. Of the hundreds of buildings, interiors, and individual articles of furniture he illustrates, he mentions the names of only two designers: the great Berlin architects Karl Friedrich Schinkel and Andreas Schlüter, and these only once each. The remainder of the works he describes only by location and date – even in instances in which noted architects were at work.

For Viennese architects and designers, like their counterparts in Germany, Folnesics and Mebes's books functioned in two ways. They served as guides to recreate "authentic" Biedermeier interiors and as sources of ideas for a new, functional form language. At first, though, most designers resisted the direct influence of Biedermeier. Hoffmann wrote in his 1901 essay "Einfache Möbel" (Simple Furniture) that he was determined to borrow the spirit, not the formal details, of *Vormärz* furniture to fashion works that were undeniably modern.[17] There was a noticeable shift in attitude in Vienna around 1904, as the Jugendstil began to lose its power and popularity. First Hoffmann, then many of his followers and others, adopted specific neoclassical motifs – sometimes directly, sometimes in highly abstracted form. These they initially incorporated into ensembles that still relied in the main on Jugendstil principles. But by the end

| Josef Hoffmann, Hall in the Palais Stoclet, Brussels, 1905–11. From *Moderne Bauformen*, special edition (Munich, 1914), p. 13.

of the first decade of the century, when Hoffmann was completing work on the Palais Stoclet (1905–11), his evocations of neoclassicism had become overt and pervasive.[18]

Some of the younger Viennese, including Oskar Strnad and Josef Frank, also made use of Biedermeier and neoclassical forms, though they did so as part of a generalized eclecticism, which mixed together freely historical imagery from a wide array of different eras and locales.[19] Yet, whatever their strategy of appropriation, the authority of *Vormärz* aesthetic culture became an essential component for many Viennese designers in the years prior to the outbreak of the war in 1914.

The reintroduction of the Biedermeier aesthetic altered, too, the Viennese modernists' perceptions of recent history. In the wake of the *Gründerzeit*, Austria's period of economic takeoff and industrialization that had commenced in the 1850s, many of Vienna's late eighteenth- and early nineteenth-century buildings were rapidly being demolished to make way for new and larger commercial structures. The rebuilding of the inner city in the years just prior to World War I threatened not only Vienna's individual Biedermeier residences and shops (the Exinger butcher shop was only one of innumerable casualties of this modernization of the city), but it also led to the removal of whole swaths of the older bourgeois urban fabric. Central to the Biedermeier revival in Vienna was an effort to save examples of architecture and interiors from the period. In the years after 1900, preservationists, supported by the modernists, rallied to protect the Franziskanerplatz, the Seitenstettengasse, and the Kornhäusel tower, among other older ensembles and buildings.[20] In their search for a new artistic truth, this younger generation of reformers emerged as the unlikely, if witting, allies of the art historians, conservationists, and social conservatives.

For Loos, the rediscovery of Vienna's Biedermeier legacy was more than a source of inspiration or an historical *cause célèbre*. It offered, he deemed, a useful guide to understanding the intricate relationship between culture and its expression.[21] Loos brought to the discussion about the aesthetic of the *Vormärz* an interest not only in its inherent modernity, but an attempt to understand how it had arisen in the first place. He focused, as he would later explain, on the nature of craft production in premodern times and its capacity for generating forms to solve everyday problems. "Twelve years ago," he remembered, "I was able to reconstruct modern joinery work."

> I did not approach the task like an artist, giving free rein to his creative imagination ... No. I went to the workshops, as timid as an apprentice, looking for the man in the blue apron. And I asked him: Share your secrets with me. For many a morsel of workshop tradition still resided there, modestly hidden from the eyes of architects ... I found modern paneling in the cladding of old lavatory water tanks; I found a modern solution for the problem of corners in silver cutlery chests; I found models for locks and metal fittings on suitcases and pianos. And I found out the most important thing: namely that the style of 1900 only differs from the style of 1800 to the same extent that a tailcoat of 1900 differs from 1800. By not very much, that is.[22]

Loos's belief that a residual and compelling modernism resided in the traditional crafts became a recurring theme in his writings. But if he shared agreement with other Austrian modernists about the need to overcome the gulf between the artistic world and everyday experience, he advocated a very different solution. For the Secessionists, the answer to this problem lay in the creation of a new, universal aesthetic – in imposing an original and total design concept. Loos assailed this position on two fronts. He rejected the prevailing belief that a new modernism would come about only when artists, architects, and designers made a full break with the past. As early as 1898, he assailed Hoffmann's quest for a novel idiom: "For me," he wrotc, "tradition is everything, the free unfolding of the imagination takes second place."[23] But Loos not only condemned the frenzied search for style; he also called into question the very concept, asserting that the Secessionists' idea of style itself was inherently flawed.[24] The problem had arisen, he argued, as industrialization began to affect architecture and design, raising the issue of a modern style.

> The second half of the nineteenth century was filled with the calls of those without culture: we have no architectural style! How wrong, how misguided. That was the very moment when we had a highly distinctive style, one that differed more clearly from the preceding period than at any time before, a change unparalleled in cultural history. But, because these false prophets could only recognize a product by the varying forms of ornamentation, ornament became a fetish for them, and they substituted it for the real thing, calling it "style."[25]

This obsession with ornament, Loos asserted, had resulted in an altered relationship with history, perverting the ways in which architects and designers had traditionally made recourse to the past.

> A true style we already had, but no ornament ... So, they kept copying from the past until even they found it laughable, and when that no longer was possible, they started inventing new ornament – which is to say, they had sunk to such a low cultural level that this was possible. And now they rejoice in having created the style of the twentieth century.[26]

Loos's solution was to graft the architecture and design of the present onto the developments of the *Vormärz*, before the corrupting influences of historicism: "So, I had to start at the point where this chain of development had been broken," he wrote. "One thing I was sure of: if I were to stay true to this line of development, I would have to aim for something considerably simpler."[27]

Loos recognized, however, that the problem of appropriation was more than a matter of formal reduction. Throughout his life, he remained steadfast in his conviction that new design solutions could only be introduced if they did not result in a loss of functionality, convenience, or a sense of permanence and tradition.[28] This latter idea was particularly important for him. He regarded changes in architecture and design as the outcome of an evolutionary process: "Everything that has been created by earlier centuries can be copied today insofar as it is still usable."[29] He dismissed the modernist belief that "changing older objects to correspond to modern needs is not allowed," contending that such an attitude was a perversion of "the natural development of our arts and crafts."[30]

The crucial problem for Loos as a practicing designer was how to remain faithful to the evolutionary spirit of the traditional crafts without imposing a new individual "artistic will." His answer was a complex one for it involved two seemingly contradictory impulses. He recognized the need to respond to the challenges of modern life: the industrial age, he acknowledged, was one of reason, objectivity, and pragmatism. Any new design would have to reflect these realities. But Loos was also unwilling to abandon the hallmarks of past design production: quality, comfort, and visual links to shared historical and cultural experience.

In his specific application of the Biedermeier aesthetic to his own work, Loos applied his strategy of sorting. He sought out those principles of early nineteenth-century design that might still be "living." Thus, he asked of each surviving object or building whether it still had meaning for the present, whether as a whole or in its parts it reflected some idea or value that might accord with life and culture in his own time. Under no circumstance did he believe that the architect or designer should merely invent something new.[31] It was the role of the architect (in contrast to the artist, whose mission it was to find novel solutions) to sublimate the desire for originality and mediate between the historical past and the present. Loos understood that this task would, of necessity, require diverse and pertinent methods. Accordingly, he conducted his sorting process in varied ways, relying in some cases on imitating or modifying direct models, in others, on altering them. His differing approaches determined not only how he borrowed from the past but the specific look of designs.

When Loos began work on his first important commission, a commercial and residential building for the tailor firm Goldman & Salatsch on the Michaelerplatz in Vienna's inner city, in 1909, he took his cue, as he explained in his essay "Architektur" (Architecture), from Biedermeier precedents.

> I saw how our ancestors built, and I saw how, century by century, year by year, they had liberated themselves from ornament ... The building had to look unobtrusive. Had I not once written that he who is dressed in a modern way is the one who draws the least attention to himself.[32]

The overall cast of the building, in point of fact, drew directly from the stripped neoclassicism of the adjacent Michaelerkirche, the front façade of which had been remodeled in the later eighteenth century. Loos did more than borrow from the simplified masses, proportions, and detailing of the church: he took some of the elements directly from it and other existing Viennese buildings. The four massive Tuscan columns that frame the entrance mimic not only the church's portico; they also strongly resembled the columns of other Biedermeier buildings in the city. Loos did nothing to alter the columns, using them instead as "readymades"– as finished components taken over without alteration or adjustment.

He had provided an explanation for this stratagem years before in his essay "Möbel" (Furniture).

> I believe that one can show if not honor then deep respect for an old master by leaving his works untouched ... We may copy old

Adolf Loos, Goldman & Salatsch Building, Vienna, 1909–11, with the church of St. Michael visible on the right. Postcard, ca. 1911. Private collection.

Adolf Loos, façade of Goldman & Salatsch Building, Vienna, 1909–11. From: *Charakteristische Details von ausgeführten Bauten* (Berlin, n.d. [ca. 1911]), n.p.

Portal of a Biedermeier house in Nußdorf. From Hartwig Fischel, *Wiener Häuser*, vol. 1 (Berlin and Vienna, 1923), n.p.

> works, copy them strictly, as precisely as is possible in our time, even to the point of giving up one's own personality. But to those who knowingly violate the old, let us cry energetically, "*hands off!*" (emphasis and English in the original).[33]

Loos's assault on those who willfully altered the ideas of the masters was a not very subtle poke at the historicists. It also underscored another important idea for him, his conviction that the conditions of modern life had changed the way new design could be made.

> In many circles, the fact that I advocate copying will meet with disapproval. Other centuries did not copy. The practice has been reserved for our century. Copying, the imitation of old stylistic forms (*Stilformen*), is a result of our social conditions, which have nothing in common with the social conditions of previous centuries.[34]

The new age, Loos explained, was the time of the bourgeoisie, whose aspirations and lifestyle contrasted markedly with the old aristocracy. Biedermeier, the first full expression of middle-class values, offered, in its advocacy of the simple and practical, a path toward a genuine and appropriate *Wohnkultur* (living culture). To repeat the styles and forms of Biedermeier sobriety was to employ history in the service of cultural continuity. Hence Loos's façade for the Anglo-Österreichische Bank (later, renamed the Zentralsparkasse der Gemeinde Wien, 1914), with its straightforward arrangement and smoothed and reduced classical pilasters, was an affirmation of the tradition of middle-class urbanity and self-esteem.

Loos maintained that reclaiming past forms also served to satisfy our need to retain a connection with the past, to offer an outlet for nostalgic desire. The purpose of repeating old forms was not only to retain their functional and practical aspects but also to allow us to reconnect with history. The act of making replicas further supported those still practicing the traditional crafts; to demand the making of high-quality replicas, as Loos knew very well, was to aid in the furtherance of handicraft and support the artisans who practiced these trades.[35]

But the direct copying of past forms, Loos recognized, had its inherent limitations. Despite his unshakable faith in tradition, he believed that the forms of the past would at times need to be adapted to meet contemporary requirements and reflect the evolution of culture over the years. Throughout his career, he

Adolf Loos, façade of the Anglo-Österreichische Bank (later, Zentralsparkasse der Gemeinde Wien), Vienna, 1914. From *Festschrift zum Jubiläum des 25jährigen Bestandes des Kredit-Vereins der Zentral-Sparkasse der Gemeinde Wien* (Vienna, 1936), after p. 8.

reexamined older objects and architectural elements, modifying them to bring them up to date. A comparison of two armoires, one a Biedermeier work illustrated in Mebes's *Um 1800*, the other, Loos's design for a related piece from the Turnovsky Apartment (1902), underscores his desire to retain the essence of the originals while updating them. Though Loos did not use the Mebes armoire – or indeed, any other specific Biedermeier armoire – as his direct model, he distilled out the essence of such objects and trimmed away those features that no longer seemed necessary. What was left retained the basic formal attributes of the *Vormärz* originals, as well as the underlying crafts techniques that had been used to fabricate them. But the piece was now remade in a modern way.

A small round table with a triangular base Loos used in the Kraus Apartment (1905) and several other commissions is a product of a closely related process of appropriation. Once more, Loos quotes from Biedermeier and neoclassical originals. Each part of the table, however – its top, legs, and base – have undergone meticulous refinement. The table's top has been smoothed and its traditional moldings have been removed; the legs have been both tapered and attenuated; and the base has been reduced. The table still bears a close relationship with the Biedermeier and neoclassical prototypes, but it is a distinct object, with its own identity.

| Armoire from Schloss Fürstenberg, ca. 1820. From Paul Mebes, *Um 1800*, vol. 2 (Munich, 1908), p. 146.

| Adolf Loos, armoire from the Turnovsky Apartment, 1902, maple with brass hardware, 130 x 59 x 201 cm. Musée d'Orsay, Paris.

| Adolf Loos, gentlemen's room in the Kraus Apartment, Vienna, 1905. Adolf Loos Archiv, Albertina, Vienna.

| Adolf Loos, table from the Manz Bookstore, Vienna, 1912, mahogany and marble, diameter 80 cm, height 65 cm. Private collection.

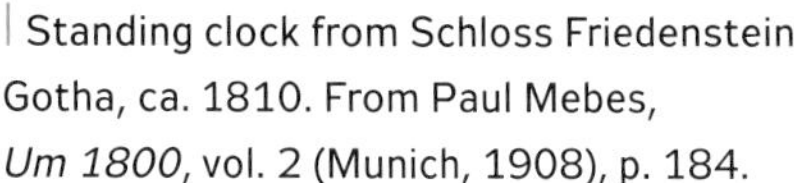

Standing clock from Schloss Friedenstein, Gotha, ca. 1810. From Paul Mebes, *Um 1800*, vol. 2 (Munich, 1908), p. 184.

Adolf Loos, mantle clock, ca. 1903, brass and glass, 38 x 26 x 48.5 cm. Dorotheum, Vienna.

The same process is manifest in Loos's design for a small mantle clock from around 1903. It, too, preserves the spirit of Biedermeier timepieces, such as the standing clock from Schloss Friedenstein in Gotha (ca. 1810) illustrated in Mebes's book. Here, though, he carried out his tactic of reduction with greater force. He maintained the basic lines of the originals while radically clarifying the form, opening up the case with glass and paring away the ornament. The new clock still speaks about a connection with the pre-March era, but it is a resolutely contemporary design.

Loos's mode of formal appropriation is not always as explicit. At times, he strove to recreate the spirit of the past, without relying directly on an earlier example. His design for the billiard space in the Café Museum (1899) departs considerably in formal terms from similar Biedermeier rooms. What he takes from such ensembles is their inherent clarity, openness, and forthrightness. He opted – aside from the billiard table itself – for light, movable furnishings, casually arranged. In this way, the space admitted a multiplicity of functions while sustaining a sense of order.

Over the next three decades, Loos continued to engage both replication and appropriation of *Vormärz* elements as design devices. In many instances, he

Adolf Loos, Café Museum with the billiard space on the left, Vienna, 1899. Adolf Loos Archiv, Albertina, Vienna.

blended the two techniques. The salon in the Strasser House in Vienna (1918–19), for instance, makes literal quotations from the Biedermeier aesthetic. (The settee, the vitrine, the marble column, parquet floor, and the classicially inspired moldings are all direct borrowings.) But his design continues the larger idea of early nineteenth-century space-making. The constitutive elements – employed as ready-mades – have been combined with a novel spatial idea, Loos's *Raumplan*, or space-plan, his notion of breaking up the regular horizontal layering of interior spaces to foster different living zones. The result is a variant form of appropriation, in which a Biedermeier interior is conjoined to a radically different spatial conception, both updating and altering the historical form.

More often, though, Loos sought merely to distill out the inner logic of pre-March arrangements, revising their forms to render them modern while conserving their aesthetic and functional coherence. One can see this process at work in the sitting corner of the Duschnitz House in Vienna (1915). Aside from

Adolf Loos, salon in the Strasser House, Vienna, 1918–19. Adolf Loos Archiv, Albertina, Vienna.

Adolf Loos, sitting corner in the Duschnitz House, Vienna, 1915. Adolf Loos Archiv, Albertina, Vienna.

the form of the vitrines, the elliptical details in the mullions of the bookcase, and the shape of the table, there are no exact repetitions of the Biedermeier form-language. The grouping, however, reproduces quite accurately the Biedermeier idea of a *Wohninsel* – literally, a living island – the practice popular at the time of informally clustering together varied types of seating with a table to create an activity center within a larger space. The heterogeneity of the individual pieces is intended to foster the idea of an ad hoc arrangement, to underline the casual basis for such social interaction. Here, as he often did, Loos employed both newly designed furnishings and pieces the clients had previously owned to emphasize

the image of a living, evolving culture. The Duschnitz salon represents a sophisticated and total appropriation, recapturing Biedermeier sensibility and practice while using novel and divergent means.

In this critical spirit, Loos worked as architect and designer on his quest for a living and suitable modern idiom. Still, he was not always content, despite his attacks on "artists" like Hoffmann, to rely solely on past models. One of his principal concerns resided in the notion, as Swiss historian Hubert Locher describes, "of promoting a sense of personal responsibility for the continued development of culture."[36] He recognized that new problems would necessitate new solutions.[37]

Nowhere in his writings, however, does Loos address directly the process of creation. He offers instead only a series of cautionary statements and admonitions. The aim in design, he insisted, rests in not giving into one's own visions or ideas, but in finding precedents to build upon. Nonetheless, Loos rarely relied entirely either on mimesis or appropriation. At times, in fact, he radically transformed earlier prototypes, converting and reshaping them in ways that departed markedly from the originals. It was through this process of transformation that he was able to act both as an agent for the new and remain within the boundaries of an evolutionary framework.

In Loos's work, the process of transformation, as with his tactic of appropriation, assumed two guises: the transformation of formal elements and the transformation of an underlying compositional logic. A resonant example of the former is the table he designed for the Kärntner Bar in Vienna (1908). It is based on the heavy pedestal tables of the *Vormärz* era, which were employed frequently as the centerpiece in salons or boudoirs. Loos's Kärntner Bar table repeats all of the basic features of such models – the large base, columnar shaft, flaring capital, and banded top. Each of these, though, has been recast. In his version, the feet have been diminished and converted to brass; the shaft support has been squared; the capital block had been enlarged and reshaped; the top has been converted from a circle (or ellipse) to an octagon; and glass and brass have replaced the traditional wood surfaces. What Loos presented was a table that still could be understood as a classically inspired object, but one with an overriding allegiance to modernist design principles.

Loos often relied on such remaking of individual features for his furniture designs. But he also transformed Biedermeier models – especially forms and spaces – by discerning their inner spirit and refashioning them. This is the second of his transformative strategies. Loos's dining room in the Villa Karma in Clarens,

Salon in Schloss Belvedere, Weimar, ca. 1810. From Paul Mebes, *Um 1800*, vol. 2 (Munich, 1908), p. 141.

Adolf Loos, table from the Kärntner Bar, Vienna, 1908, mahogany, brass, and glass, 55.5 x 29.5 x 68 cm. Private collection.

Switzerland (1903–06), suggests both a distillation and transformation of earlier, neoclassical interiors. Only two of the room's features – the checkerboard floor and the French doors – evoke pure associations with late eighteenth- and early nineteenth-century rooms. Everything else, from the smooth marble walls to the built-in sideboard, is, in fact, new. The rounded-over divider between the doors resembles a standard pilaster; its execution and scale, however, have been modified. Loos has also compressed the zone between the tops of the walls and the ceiling, removing the cornice or moldings, and he has flattened the remaining walls, relying on the patterning of the marble to achieve an ornamental effect. The ceiling, a direct application of Gottfried Semper's *Bekleidung* theory, relates to the traditional application of leather but is a modern conception, well removed from classical ceiling treatments. The same is true of the clerestory window and the proportions of the credenza below, which would have normally been executed in wood rather than stone. Where Loos had to insert a modern innovation, such as the light fixtures in the room, he opted, just as he had suggested, for modern products available on the market. The result is an ensemble that is resolutely of Loos's making. It is a thorough reimagining of such spaces.

If the adaptation and willful reshaping of Biedermeier forms was a shared response to the problem of a modern style for many of the early Central European modernists, they did so with widely differing aims. What set Loos apart from his contemporaries was not so much the specific look of his designs – the formal differences between the majority of his Biedermeier-influenced works and those of Hoffmann, as I noted before, are not as large as one might first assume – but his steadfast commitment to a rigorous process of sorting. Loos's rejection of the imperatives of artistic invention led him on another course: to retain consciously as much of the knowledge of the old masters as possible. He never shed his conviction that design was an evolutionary process – that the modern designer could only find a modern style through the refinement of what had come before. His understanding of the trajectory of the recent culture led him to believe that simplicity and practicality were the dominant trends of the new age, and that the role of the architect was to sift through and reprocess the forms of the past. His ultimate rejection of modern ornament was born of this belief.

In the end, Loos's modernism, for all of its prescience, remained just outside the modernist mainstream. In the years after World War I, when most of the avant-garde rejected the notion of historical continuity in favor of a purified and intentionally ahistorical aesthetic, Loos continued to argue that architects and designers could find the basis for a modern expression in the past. Unlike the

Adolf Loos, dining room in the Villa Karma, Clarens, Switzerland, 1903–06. Adolf Loos Archiv, Albertina, Vienna.

other early modernists, whose interest in the *Vormärz* proved to be fleeting, Loos's embrace of the Biedermeier was not a temporary measure but part of a larger understanding of his place in the course of cultural evolution. His faith in precedent, though, diverged from that of the historicists. If Loos, too, mined the past for ideas, he did so with an ardent respect for the achievements of the artists and craftspeople of previous times. He saw his work as an attempt to preserve the spirit and culture of the past, not as a striving to recreate or surpass it. What had been handed down to him from the Biedermeier era, he thought, was a legacy to be diligently maintained and continued.

4 | Trotzdem

When Adolf Loos published *Trotzdem*, in 1931, he was sixty years old and in failing health. Two years later, after several strokes, he died alone, a broken and resigned man, in a private sanitarium outside Vienna. It was an inglorious ending for an architect whose mythic stature has come nearly to overshadow his achievements and one at odds with Loos's own sense of his place in history. In the preface to his book, Loos had declared victory in his "thirty-year-long struggle . . . to free mankind from excessive ornament. 'Ornament,'" he wrote, "was once the epithet for 'beautiful.' Today, thanks to my life's work, it is the epithet for 'mediocre.'"[1] Even the book's title, which might best be translated as "Nevertheless," was an avowal of his long fight and a pronouncement of triumph. It derives from a passage by Nietzsche that Loos quotes at the beginning of the preface: "Das entscheidende geschieht trotzdem," or "What is decisive happens nevertheless."

Trotzdem was Loos's second book. The first, *Ins Leere gesprochen* (Spoken into the Void), which had appeared in 1921, reprinted his writings up to the year 1900, including the series of brilliant reviews he published in the *Neue Freie Presse*, Austria's leading daily newspaper.[2] *Trotzdem* incorporates most of Loos's

ADOLF LOOS

TROTZDEM

1900—1930

MCMXXXI
BRENNER-VERLAG, INNSBRUCK

| Adolf Loos, title page from the first edition of *Trotzdem* (Innsbruck, 1931).

later writings, covering the period from 1900 to 1930, the peak years of his architectural activity. The thirty-one essays in the book include many of his best-known texts, among them "Ornament und Verbrechen" (Ornament and Crime), "Die Überflüssigen" (The Superfluous Ones), "Architektur" (Architecture), "Josef Veillich," "Heimatkunst" (Vernacular Art), and "Ornament und Erziehung" (Ornament and Education).[3] With the exception of "Aus meinem Leben" (From My Life), "Kulturentartung" (Cultural Degeneration), and "Kleines Intermezzo" (A Small Intermezzo), all of the essays had been published previously, most in daily newspapers in Austria, or in progressive German-language culture magazines. Yet while *Ins Leere gesprochen* has been translated into English, there is still no complete translation of *Trotzdem*, though several of the essays are included in *Ornament and Crime: Selected Essays*, a compilation of Loos's writings edited by Adolf Opel, which appeared in 1998.[4] The absence of a translation is all the more glaring because *Trotzdem* is without question the more important of the two books: it contains not only Loos's mature statements of his beliefs about architecture and design, but it also presents his rejoinders to his critics and his explanations of his intentions for several of his most significant buildings.

But *Trotzdem* is more than a guide to Loos's works and ideas. Anyone who has read Loos in the original is immediately aware of his remarkable facility as a writer. No other architect in the German-speaking lands at the time wrote with such simple eloquence. It is no exaggeration to say that Loos was as concerned with writing as he was with building; that the closest friends of his early years, Karl Kraus and Peter Altenberg, were both writers says much about his preoccupation. What distinguishes Loos's prose is not only its immediacy – his writings were always directed at a general audience, not solely at architects and designers –but also its clarity and economy. There are few wasted words, even fewer stray thoughts. His friend Otto Stoessl once compared Loos's "concise, conversational style" with Voltaire's language: "beautifully pure, like cold spring water."[5] No English translation has quite captured his pellucid style–or his acid wit. Indeed, as a writer and thinker, Loos has a great deal more in common with H. L. Mencken than with Le Corbusier; his relentless cultural criticism is wrapped in nearly equal amounts of caustic satire, ethical indignation, and broad humor.

As a book, *Trotzdem* was never especially successful. First published by a small press that specialized in contemporary Austrian literature, it found only a limited readership when it originally appeared, and the work languished in obscurity for the next three decades, until Loos was rediscovered in the early 1960s.[6] The scant interest the book first encountered was no doubt related to its timing. In the late 1920s, Loos was becoming a forgotten figure: his work and ideas were out of step with the reigning spirit of *Sachlichkeit*, and the younger modernists in Germany regarded him as démodé. It was only with the publication of "Ornament and Crime" and several other essays in the *Frankfurter Zeitung* in 1929 and the appearance of *Trotzdem* the following year that Loos again found a wider audience.[7] In the mid-1930s, however, Nikolaus Pevsner could still write: "Loos is one of the greatest creators in modern architecture. In spite of that, he never became known, during his lifetime, to more than a small circle of admirers. His influence remained negligible for a long time. All the other pioneers [of modern architecture] were more widely discussed and imitated."[8]

With the rise of the Nazis in Germany, the discourse on modernism in Central Europe was silenced. It would take another two decades for Loos's contribution to be fully recognized. The Loos revival, which began in the early 1960s, was spawned by the publication of Ludwig Münz and Gustav Künstler's *Der Architekt Adolf Loos*, and the first of two announced volumes of Loos's complete writings, edited by Franz Glück.[9] The latter work, which included the full texts of *Ins Leere gesprochen* and *Trotzdem*, made Loos's writings widely available for the first time. Some years ago, both books were republished by Georg Prachner Verlag in Vienna, and more recently a complete edition of all of Loos's writings has appeared.[10]

But Loos, it seems – at least in the English-speaking world – is still more frequently quoted than read. All too often Loos is identified as an unrepentant functionalist, or worse, as an early twentieth-century Savonarola who purged architecture of all of its alleged impurities. Le Corbusier's oft-repeated dictum that Loos had given architecture "a Homeric cleansing" has only served to bolster his undeserved reputation as a wild-eyed ascetic. Loos is not without blame in fostering his myth: his penchant for dramatic overstatement sometimes obscured his ideas. The mere title "Ornament and Crime," is, as Loos intended, a provocation. Yet even a casual reading of the essay reveals – in contradiction to what is so often claimed – that he never asserts that ornament *is* crime or that he calls for the eradication of *all* ornament. What Loos writes instead is this: "I have discovered the following truth and passed it on to the world: *the evolution of culture is synonymous with the removal of ornament from objects of daily use* (evolution der kultur ist gleichbedeutend mit dem entfernen des ornaments aus dem gebrauchsgegenstande)."[11]

Loos did not call for the removal of ornament from monumental architecture: rather, he recognized that ornament would slowly disappear over time. For many of the modernists of the 1920s, who read their own intentions into Loos's text, his words seemed to provide an explicit defense for the abolition of ornament. Years later, in 1924, in "Ornament and Education," Loos attempted to clarify his position: "Twenty-six years ago, I argued that the use of ornament would disappear with the development of humankind, a constant and consistent development, which was as natural as the process of dropping vowels at the ends of words in ordinary speech. I never meant, as the purists have repeated *ad absurdum*, that ornament should be systematically and consistently eliminated. What I meant was that where ornament had disappeared as a consequence of human development it can no longer be used, just as people will never return to tattooing their faces."[12]

One is left to wonder how the misunderstanding could have arisen at all, if anyone had read "Ornament and Crime." The answer is that almost no one in the German-speaking world had seen the text prior to the end of the 1920s.[13] Although Loos first presented "Ornament and Crime" as a lecture in 1910 – possibly in 1909 – and repeated it a number of times afterward, it was not published until 1913, in French, in *Les cahiers d'aujourd'hui*, in a translation by Marcel Ray.[14] Le Corbusier included Ray's translation of the essay in the second issue of *L'Esprit nouveau* in November 1920,[15] and the same version of the text also appeared in *L'architecture vivante* in 1926.[16] The essay was not published in German, however, until October 1929, in the *Frankfurter Zeitung*.[17] But by then the myth of Loos as the slayer of ornament had grown up, and the subsequent appearance of the essay in *Trotzdem* did little to correct the misunderstanding.

Lost, too, in the current barrage of critical texts on Vienna and design at the turn of the century (which persistently cite, and also misrepresent, Loos's views on a wide variety of topics) is the down-to-earth quality of his writing. His essays are always insightful and probing – sometimes even remarkably prescient – but they are not the work of a deeply intellectual thinker. Loos did not possess the critical ability of, say, his younger contemporaries Walter Benjamin and Hannah Arendt; he was instead a keen observer of the everyday, who proved extraordinarily adept at converting his own consternation about what he saw into a practical philosophy. Loos's great gift was an ability to convey, in simple and direct fashion, the meaning of the changes he witnessed, and to propose alternatives.

Most of Loos's essays were particular to the Vienna of his time. Although they transcend reportage, there is often a distinctly journalistic flavor to his writing. It is also true that Loos's perceptions and his judgments in matters of taste are no longer those of our time: his conviction that tattoos could only be the

ORNAMENT UND VERBRECHEN

(1908)

Der menschliche embryo macht im mutterleibe alle entwicklungsphasen des tierreiches durch. Wenn der mensch geboren wird, sind seine sinneseindrücke gleich denen eines neugeborenen hundes. Seine kindheit durchläuft alle wandlungen, die der geschichte der menschheit entsprechen. Mit zwei jahren sieht er wie ein papua, mit vier jahren wie ein germane, mit sechs jahren wie Sokrates, mit acht jahren wie Voltaire. Wenn er acht jahre alt ist, kommt ihm das violett zum bewußtsein, die farbe, die das achtzehnte jahrhundert entdeckt hat, denn vorher waren das veilchen blau und die purpurschnecke rot. Der physiker zeigt heute auf farben im sonnenspektrum, die bereits einen namen haben, deren erkenntnis aber dem kommenden menschen vorbehalten ist.

Das kind ist amoralisch. Der papua ist es für uns auch. Der papua schlachtet seine feinde ab und verzehrt sie. Er ist kein verbrecher. Wenn aber der moderne mensch jemanden abschlachtet und verzehrt, so ist er ein verbrecher oder ein degenerierter. Der papua tätowiert seine haut, sein boot, sein ruder, kurz alles was ihm erreichbar ist. Er ist kein verbrecher. Der moderne mensch, der sich tätowiert, ist ein verbrecher oder ein degenerierter. Es gibt gefängnisse, in denen achtzig prozent der häftlinge tätowierungen aufweisen. Die tätowierten, die nicht in haft sind, sind latente verbrecher oder degenerierte aristokraten. Wenn ein

Loos 81 6

| First page of "Ornament and Crime" in the first edition of *Trotzdem* (Innsbruck, 1931), p. 81.

mark of criminals and degenerates, for instance, is contradicted by the current fashion for body art. To suggest, however, as Adolf Opel has, that "what is needed today is a selection of his writings which omits those dealing with out-of-date, peripheral, or transient matters," is to miss some of the import of his essays: it is in their potential for revealing the concerns of Loos's day – their very historicity, in other words – that their meaning partly resides.[18] In "Aus meinem Leben" (From My Life), for instance, Loos writes:

> I met the famous modern interior designer X. on the street.
> Good day, I say, yesterday I saw an apartment of yours.
> Uh huh, which one was it?
> The one for Dr. Y.
> Oh, the one for Dr. Y. For heaven's sake, don't look at that piece of crap. I did it three years ago.
> What, you say! I always thought, my dear colleague, that our differences were on matters of principle. Now I see that we just disagree on time. It is a difference that one can even express in years. Three years! I said even then that it was a piece of crap–and it took you until today.[19]

The piece is, in part, a blunt assault on the Jugendstil and its makers. It is also about the transitory nature of fashion, which assumes rapid obsolescence. Loos's most trenchant observation, which is repeated in many of his early writings, however, involves the formation of modernity. The clue in the text is Loos's use of the word *Raumkünstler*, which may be translated as "interior designer," but would more literally be rendered as "room artist" or "space artist." Here Loos intended the term as a pejorative. The design of interiors – in fact, the design of all objects of daily use – should not, he avowed, lie in the sphere of art, but rather in that of craft. The tendency to confuse art, which entailed making objects for contemplation, with handicraft, which involved fabricating what should merely be useful (albeit attractive), was a symptom of what was wrong with modern design. A genuine modern style, Loos believed, would arise on its own; one only had to look to the anonymous products of ordinary craftsmen to find it. Lina Loos, Loos's first wife, remembered that one of his prized possessions when she first met him was a Russian cigarette case: made of polished birch, which "allowed the natural ornamental beauty of the wood to emerge," it expressed "its beauty only through the functionality of its form."[20]

The notion that natural forms and materials are in themselves beautiful runs through Loos's writings. *"Precious materials"* (italics in the original), he wrote in "Hands Off" in 1917, *"are God's miracle.* I would gladly trade all of Lalique's art works or all of the jewelry of the Wiener Werkstätte for a good string of pearls."[21] Yet Loos also valued man-made ornament – provided it was appropriate. In "Josef Veillich" (1929), an obituary of his beloved cabinetmaker who produced many of the Chippendale chairs and other historical reproductions Loos incorporated into his interiors, he complained that the problem was not ornament per se, but the ability to "clearly and cleanly differentiate between art and handicraft." The Chippendale chair retained its validity in the modern age – despite its ornamental detailing – because it was a "perfect" example of the craftsman's art and because it was still usable.[22]

A close reading of this and other texts also offers telling insight into Loos's design process. Indeed, one of the striking features of Loos's writings is their consistency. While it is possible to discern a certain development of his thought, Loos had already articulated his basic design philosophy in the late 1890s, and his views changed little over the next three decades. And perhaps just as remarkable, if one compares the writings of many other twentieth-century architects, his writings correlate quite exactly with his architectural work. What Loos wrote is also what he built: his own ethical stance would not have permitted him to do otherwise.

In "Zwei Aufsätze und eine Zuschrift über das Haus auf dem Michaelerplatz" (Two Essays and an Addendum on the House in the Michaelerplatz, 1910), for example, Loos describes in clear and direct fashion each aspect of the building's design and its underlying logic. The decision to clad the lower floors (housing an exclusive tailor salon) in marble and the upper portion of the building (intended for apartments) in stucco resulted from their differing functions. The choice of materials in either case was determined by the traditions of Viennese building. The plastered surface of the upper stories was a response to the older bourgeois buildings of the inner city. The interior of the shop, on the other hand, "required a modern solution. The old masters left us with no models for a modern retail establishment. The same is true for modern lighting fixtures. If they were to rise from their graves, they would soon find a solution, however. Not in the way the so-called modernists do. And certainly not as do the older architects [of our time], who stick porcelain candles with lightbulbs into antique candleholders. They would instead make something entirely new – and very different from what these two opposing camps think they would."[23]

This idea of a modernism rooted in traditional modes of production is perhaps the most salient – and from today's vantage, also the most arresting – of *Trotzdem's* recurring themes. Oskar Kokoschka, a close friend of Loos, recalled that among Loos's prized possessions was an early Italian edition of Vitruvius. It was Loos's "Bible," he wrote, providing him with a guide to "the appropriate handling of the material" and "the use of architectural elements."[24] "Our culture," Loos insisted in his essay "Architecture" (1910), "is erected on the unsurpassed greatness of classical antiquity. Our mode of thinking and our sensibilities are taken over from the Romans. From the Romans, too, come our social perceptions and intellectual cultivation."[25]

But Loos found his way to modernism not only through a reconsideration of the past: he also engaged in an intense questioning of the changing world around him. At the core of *Trotzdem* – indeed, of all of Loos's writings and works – is a striving to draw exact distinctions: between what from the past was still living and what was not, between what belonged to the sphere of art and what was the province of the everyday, between what was genuine and what was contrived. And it is in this process of sorting that Loos's lesson for our time resides. In "Architecture," he wrote: "The art of building (*Baukunst*) has, through the actions of architects, deteriorated to the level of graphic art. No longer is the one who can build best the one who receives the most commissions, but, rather, the one who does the best work on paper. And these two are antipodes."[26]

In a similar way, Loos also argued that we have come to lose sight of what architecture is ultimately about: "Architecture arouses feelings in people. The task for the architect therefore is to frame these feelings precisely. A living room should be comfortable, a house appear livable. A courthouse must look threatening to those contemplating crime. A bank must say: here your money is being held in safe-keeping by honest people."[27]

In an age when schools all too often look like prisons, and suburban houses aspire to the monumentality of palaces, such advice seems all the more timely.

5 | A Private Portrait

When Claire Beck (Klára Becková) married Adolf Loos in the summer of 1929, he was nearly sixty and in fading health. He was still working; in fact, he was then engaged with what would later be acknowledged as several of his seminal designs. The Villa Müller in Prague, the culmination of his two-decades-long experiment with spatial planning ideas, was under construction, and he had other important works on the boards or in progress, among them the Khuner House in the village of Payerbach in Lower Austria and a project for a house for Hugo and Lisa Bojko in Vienna. Craftspeople were also completing various interiors he had created for clients in Pilsen, in Czechoslovakia, where he had long been active as a designer.

Claire Beck was the daughter of another of his patrons in Pilsen, Otto Beck, who was co-owner, with his cousin Wilhelm (Willy) Hirsch (yet another of Loos's clients there), of the Pilsen Wire and Nail Works. She was only twenty-four. Her father, just two years older than Loos, was adamantly opposed to the marriage and refused to give his blessing, but Claire persisted, and after hasty arrangements, the two were wed in Vienna, with only Claire's mother, Loos's maid, and a few others in attendance. The marriage was a disaster: the two separated in 1931, and they divorced the following year. Loos died a short time later, in 1933.

| Claire Beck (Klára Becková) and Adolf Loos clowning at their wedding. From left to right: Mitzi Schnabl, Loos's housekeeper; unidentified man; Claire Beck; Adolf Loos; Heinrich Kulka, Loos's assistant; and Claire's mother Olga Beck. Vienna, July 18, 1929. Courtesy of Carrie Paterson.

The whole episode might have remained scarcely more than a footnote in Loos's biography had not Claire Loos (she insisted on keeping his surname after their divorce, presenting herself that way, or, in Czech, as Klára Becková Loosová) published a little book in 1936, *Adolf Loos Privat*, a series of telling vignettes about Loos and their all too brief life together. The work here under review is the first English translation of that work, augmented with several texts and family photographs by Carrie Paterson, Claire's great-niece, who lives in Los Angeles.

The original book, small in format, runs a little more than 160 pages and is divided into brief, discrete chapters, most no more than two or three pages in length. Each is titled and relates a brief story about some moment or exchange in Loos's life of those years, episodes in nearly every instance that Claire Loos witnessed in person. Most of the chapters fall into one of several categories. Among these are incidents that underline Loos's ideas. He once berates his young wife, for example, for wasting soap: "Don't you know," he cries at her, "that I have spent my entire life fighting against the senseless, against ornamentation, against the

CLAIRE LOOS

ADOLF LOOS PRIVAT

VERLAG DER JOHANNES-PRESSE

WIEN 1936

| Title of Claire Beck Loos's book *Adolf Loos Privat* (Vienna, 1936).

waste of energy, against the waste of material."[1] There are also chapters that illustrate well Loos's character, his insouciance in matters of money (Claire wonders one day why he has no bank account; he responds that money is to be spent, nothing more), his often gruff manner with those around him (he frequently scolds her, his assistants, and his clients), his intransigence in questions of design, and his admitted anti-Semitism (in spite of the fact that most of his friends, two of his three wives, and many of his assistants and students were Jewish).[2]

What makes the book most valuable is the fine-grained portrait it provides us of Loos's last years, of his activities and his preoccupations. In the chapter on the Villa Müller, for instance, Claire Loos writes, "The Müller house is growing. Loos orders an overhang of half a centimeter on the house. He drives away. When he returns, the overhang measures an entire centimeter instead of only a half. Loos is beside himself and has the extra half a centimeter taken off all the way around the house."[3] (One is reminded here of Ludwig Wittgenstein – an architectural protege of sorts of Loos – having a similar exchange with his builder concerning the house he built for his sister on the Kundmanngasse in Vienna.) But Loos always has clearly expressed reasons, as Claire discovers, for what seem at first glance to be rather capricious decisions. She wonders aloud about the small size of the dining room in the Müller house. He replies, "It is large enough as long as the maid can comfortably serve the meal. There is no need for more room than that."[4] The kitchen, too, she finds, is "surprisingly small." She soon learns the reason: "Cooking is done here following the American system. Everything is within easy reach and has its own designated place. Loos uses the kitchen of a dining car as a model. A light is installed above the stove. The window is high. Loos explains, smiling: '[I]t is unnecessary for the cook to be able to look out of the window while cooking.'"[5]

But Claire also discovers that Loos at times gives into flights of pure fantasy. During a stay in Nice, she observes that he spends a great deal of time searching for property on which to build: "He never tires of looking over property with the agents. Calculations are made, measurements taken, bartering done. Dead tired, but healthy as never before, he returns at lunchtime. I dare once to softly ask a question: 'Dolfi how can any of this end well? We do not have any money!' He looks disappointed. Defiant like a child who is about to have his favorite toy taken away, he replies: 'How can you spoil the enjoyment I am getting from working on this project by asking that, Lerle! Didn't I tell you we have to be ready for when the rich financier shows up?!' Irritated, he leaves me; soon he has built the entire Riviera in his head."[6]

The marriage ended unhappily. Loos's intransigence and continual verbal abuse of his wife, the latter a symptom of what could only be characterized as mounting paranoia (very probably the result, it seems, of tertiary syphilis), were the chief reasons. Toward the end of her book, Claire Loos relates one anecdote that exemplifies the growing friction between them. It concerns a letter Loos received from one of his assistants, Norbert Krieger, also from Pilsen. Krieger wrote to Loos informing him that one of their clients wanted Krieger to design a project for him. Krieger told Loos, "Since I am working for you, I didn't accept. What should I do?" The letter angered Loos. When Claire defends Krieger, he charges her with betrayal and sends her away, exclaiming, "[L]eave me alone!-–You will cause me more grief than Josef Hoffmann, my worst enemy!"[7] After the divorce, she saw him once more, on his deathbed following a major stroke. He is pleased to see her and immediately plans a trip with her, which both know is no longer possible. As she departs, she writes, he was "sitting up straight in the wheelchair, motionless. He does not speak, he does not wave, he looks towards me."[8]

Claire Loos survived her husband by less than a decade. As Carrie Paterson tells us in the afterword, she and her mother were interned at Terezín (Theresienstadt) in 1941; in early 1942, she was deported to Riga and was killed almost immediately upon arrival there. She was thirty-seven.

The English translation of her book, made by Constance C. Pontasch and Nicholas Saunders, is fluent and accurate, conveying well the tone of Claire Loos's original (which, in turn, to some extent mimics Loos's own writing style). Paterson's introduction and afterword, along with some forty previously unpublished family photographs, add to the story and help flesh it out. It is a richly informative, if sad, tale, and, in Claire's telling, undoubtedly a very largely truthful one.

But in a sense, it is misleading, for though it exposes Loos's many personal idiosyncrasies and faults (as well as a few of his more positive qualities), it sheds precious little light on his working method or on the true wellspring of his talents. In the end, none of the anecdotes quite reveals what lay behind his design of a work like the Villa Müller, so complete and so pregnant with architectural meaning.

6 | "Ich warne Sie vor Josef Hoffmann!"

At the beginning of his very fine essay about the contentious relationship between Adolf Loos and Josef Hoffmann, Markus Kristan relates an anecdote about the two men, from which the title of his book derives. It comes from the memoirs of the journalist Soma Morgenstern, who, in August 1933, mere days before Loos's death, went to visit him in a sanatorium in Kalksburg, just outside of Vienna. Accompanying him were the architects Josef Frank and László Gábor. Morgenstern was surprised that Loos failed to recognize any of the men, most of all Frank, who had been a long and valued friend. They were shocked at his deteriorated condition and the fact that a figure that had once had such a brilliant mind was now reduced to such a state. As a nurse sat next to Loos feeding him with a teaspoon like a small child, the three men stood on the opposite side of the room conversing in low voices. Gábor remarked: "Such an end would actually fit more to Josef Hoffmann." Loos, who up to this point had barely taken notice of his visitors, suddenly stirred. He pointed his finger at the nurse and exclaimed: "Hoffmann! – Hoffmann! – Ich warne Sie vor Josef Hoffmann!" (Hoffmann! Hoffmann! I warn you about Josef Hoffmann!)[1]

Loos's plaintive words that day were a fitting summation of his more than thirty-year-long crusade against Hoffmann, against Hoffmann's beloved Wiener

Josef Hoffmann, 1903. Photograph by Friedrich Viktor Spitzer. MAK–Österreichisches Museum für angewandte Kunst / Gegenwartskunst, Vienna.

Wiener Werkstätte showroom, Neustiftgasse 32–34, Vienna, 1910. MAK–Österreichisches Museum für angewandte Kunst / Gegenwartskunst, Vienna.

Werkstätte, and against superfluous ornament in general. Kristan's book recounts the protracted struggle between the two men, between their opposing views of ornament and, ultimately, between their differing ideas concerning the proper path to modernism. The work is divided into two sections. One, which makes up much of the book, is a compendium of nineteen published essays from the period – the great majority of them authored by Loos or Hoffmann – detailing their ideas and their attacks on each other. The second part is made up of Kristan's roughly forty-page essay about the two men and their unhappy relationship. Among the essays included are many that are not readily available elsewhere, such as Hoffmann's 1926 piece, "Meine Gegner und ich" (My Opponents and I), and Loos's 1931 article, "Modern angezogen" (Dressed in a Modern Way). It is undeniably useful to have these disparate essays collected together in a single volume, but the real value in this book rests in Kristan's essay and his meticulous recounting of the momentous quarrel between these two figures, who formed the intellectual poles of Vienna's distinctive contribution to the new architecture and design.

Loos and Hoffmann knew each other since their teens, when both had been students in the building trades department of the Staatsgewerbeschule (State Trades School) in Brünn (Brno). Both had grown up in Moravia – Loos in Brünn, Hoffmann in nearby Pirnitz (Brtnice) – and they were born in the same year, 1870. The deep-seated antagonism that would mark their relationship for decades, however, did not make its appearance until the later 1890s, after they had settled in Vienna. Indeed, as Kristan points out, Loos, in one of his very earliest writings, had been complimentary of Hoffmann's competition design for an exhibition pavilion commemorating Emperor Franz Joseph's fiftieth jubilee.[2] And after the founding of the Secession, Loos and Hoffmann collaborated on Loos's essay, "Die Potemkin'sche Stadt," which appeared in the July 1898 issue of the group's magazine *Ver Sacrum*. (Hoffmann provided a group of architectonic drawings that were paired with Loos's piece.)

Their falling out came a short time later, in November of the same year, when Loos expressed the wish to design the "Ver Sacrum room," a meeting space in the new Secession building. What transpired precisely is unclear, but we know that Hoffmann rejected the idea and that Loos was deeply wounded by his refusal. Ever after, he would be a relentless critic of Hoffmann and his work.[3] Kristan, though, contends that this incident was only the proximate cause of Loos's bitterness toward Hoffmann; their break was inevitable because of Loos's developing radical purism, "which was diametrically opposed to the ideas of the

Secession."[4] In fact, by 1898, in one of his articles for the *Neue Freie Presse*, "Das Luxusfuhrwerk" (Luxury Carriages), Loos's rejection of "superfluous" ornament was already becoming manifest. Hoffmann also contributed to the split, remarking, for example, in his 1901 article "Einfache Möbel" (Simple Furniture), that maintaining the tradition of handicraft in Vienna was no longer desirable. ("Should we want the old handicraft practices to be maintained? God forbid.") Such a view was diametrically opposed to Loos's, who thought that it was precisely the ideas and practices of the city's many traditional craftspeople that offered the best solution for generating an authentic new design culture.

The split between the two men became even more pronounced with Hoffmann and Koloman Moser's founding of the Wiener Werkstätte in May 1903. Every aspect of the company's mission troubled Loos – the striving for a totalizing, unified design concept (*Gesamtkunstwerk*), the effort to contrive a new modern language ex nihilo, and the designers' unabashed use of ornament. For nearly three decades, until 1932, when the Werkstätte was ultimately forced into bankruptcy, Loos hardly missed an opportunity to assail Hoffmann and impugn the company and all that it stood for. The matter finally came to a head in the spring of 1928, the twenty-fifth anniversary of the Werkstätte's establishment, when Loos delivered a blistering public talk – fittingly titled "Das Wiener Weh (Wiener Werkstätte) – Eine Abrechnung!" (Vienna's Woe [Wiener Werkstäte] – A Reckoning) – in which he denigrated the efforts of Hoffmann and the other Werkstätte designers as a tragic misstep in the march to a modern culture, one that was elitist, socially injurious, and misguided: "The modern spirit is a social spirit, modern objects are not only for the upper crust, but for everyone. All objects of daily use are identical with that which their form requires. In that way, they manifest themselves as modern. If they are made differently, it is false, socially inappropriate, and, therefore, not modern."[5]

Loos's unusually harsh tone – even for him – prompted the directors of the Wiener Werkstätte to publish an open letter calling on Loos to let the matter of slander be settled in court. (Because Loos was not an Austrian citizen – he had opted for Czechoslovak citizenship after World War I – he could not be tried there without his acquiescence.)[6] Even Hoffmann, who rarely spoke out publicly against Loos, published an open letter in one of the city's daily newspapers defending himself and the company: "Herr Loos is exceptionally witty and highly skilled in public speaking, which I unfortunately am not, so that in this form I cannot take up a fight with him ... It is enough for me to know, purely privately, that all of the accusations that were made against me are either untrue or off the mark."[7]

For the acutely sensitive Hoffmann, Loos's repeated attacks must have been increasingly difficult to bear. He mostly remained silent in later years. But after Loos's death he extracted a measure of revenge by working to remove Frank, Oskar Strnad, and other allies of Loos from their positions of power in the Austrian Werkbund by setting up a competing organization. And much later, in the 1950s, in a short autobiography, he made light of Loos's antagonism, writing that when Loos had designed his "American bar" on the Kärntnerdurchgang, in 1907, he and his friends had "applauded" Loos's achievement, "and those of us who went in and out there did not take his enmity entirely seriously."[8]

The long "war" between the men and their respective camps, however, characterized one of the great oppositions of the early modernist era, the struggle between "intentional design" – Hoffmann's belief in creative action and license – and Loos's notion that any design idiom must be a direct reflection of a given culture. All design, Loos held (in direct opposition to Hoffmann), is ultimately born of need and a shared *Gegenstandswollen* – to slightly twist Alois Riegl's well-known formulation. It was an early and meaningful skirmish in a conflict that remains very much a part of our own design world.

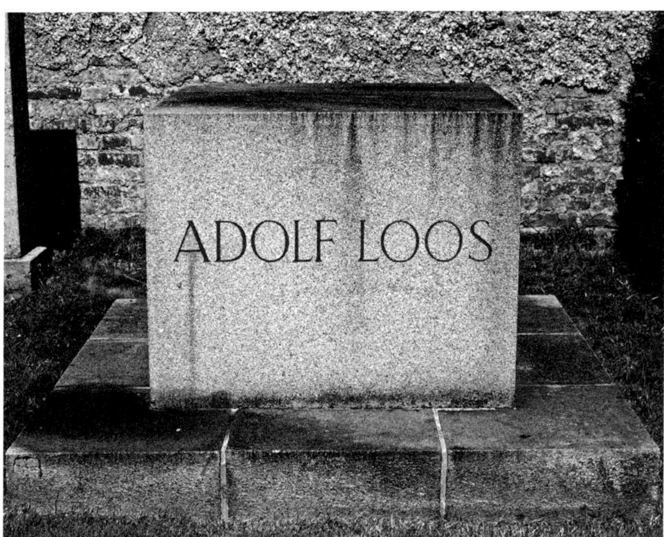

Adolf Loos's gravestone in Vienna's Central Cemetery. Private collection.

Acknowledgments

The essays in this volume represent many years of my life as a scholar and writer, and, as a consequence, the debts that I have incurred are also many. I would—first—especially like to thank the excellent editors I was fortunate to collaborate with: William S. Saunders and Nancy Levinson from their time at *Harvard Design Magazine*; Paul Stirton, editor of *West 86th: A Journal of Decorative Arts, Design History and Material Culture*; Dora Wiebenson, editor of *Centropa*; David Brownlee, former editor at the *Journal of the Society of Architectural Historians*; Sarah B. Sherrill, from her time at *Studies in the Decorative Arts*, and Pilar Parcerisas from the Museu del Disseny de Barcelona.

For assisting me with locating information and photographs, I would like to thank Maria Makela, Peter Jelavich, Sherwin Simmons, Josef Strasser, and Werner Lang. I also wish to extend my gratitude to Danielle Kovacs, Special Collections and Archives of the W. E. B. Du Bois Library, University of Massachusetts, Amherst; Markus Kristan and Ingrid Kastel, Albertina, Vienna; and Helmut Selzer, Wien Museum, Vienna. In addition, I want to express my thanks to the librarians, archivists, and staff members of the following institutions: Avery Architectural and Fine Arts Library, Columbia University, New York; New York Public Library;

Österreichische Nationalbibliothek—Bildarchiv, Vienna; Staatsbibliothek zu Berlin—Preußischerkulturbesitz, Handschriftensammlung; Architecture and Planning Library at the University of Texas at Austin; and the Wien Bibliothek, Vienna. I also want to acknowledge my very able research assistants over the years, Barbara Ellen Brown, Lauren Hamer, Laura McGuire, Natsumi Nonaka, and Kathryn Pierce. Birgit Michaelis, in Berlin, and Stefan Bader, in Munich, aided me in tracking down important sources, as did Martina Hrabova in Prague. I owe a very special debt of thanks to Elana Shapira, who helped me assemble a number of articles, photographs, and documents. Grants from the Vice President for Research and the Martin S. Kermacy Endowment of the University of Texas at Austin supported my travel and research. I want thank my colleagues Richard Cleary, Francesco Passanti, and Wilfried Wang for their thoughtful advice and assistance.

I am grateful that I could work with Wolfgang Thaler in Vienna, who made the photographs on the book's cover. I owe a significant debt to R. Scott Gill and Claudia Mazanek, who read and commented on an early draft of "Becoming Loos." I also thank Kathleen Conti, who aided me in transcribing some of the texts into digital form, and Ulrike Unterweger, who kindy proofread the text and offered many helpful suggestions.

I had the privilege and good fortune of working once again with Deborah Bruce-Hostler, who edited the English-language version of this book. I also want to extend my fond thanks to Karel Kerlický of KANT Publishers in Prague for undertaking this project, and to Jiří Příhoda for his splendid book design.

Finally, I must thank my wife, Gia Marie Houck, who contributed to this work in more ways than she will ever know.

Permissions and Credits

Portions of "Becoming Loos" were originally published as "Lessons of America," in Pilar Parcerisas, ed., *Adolf Loos: Private Spaces* (Barcelona: Museu del Disseny de Barcelona / Editorial Tenov, 2017): 22—35.

"The Origins and Context of Adolf Loos's "Ornament and Crime" was published in *Journal of the Society of Architectural Historians* 68, no. 2 (June 2009): 200–23.

"Adolf Loos and the Biedermeier Revival in Vienna" was published in *Centropa* 10, no. 2 (May 2010): 128–40.

"Adolf Loos's *Trotzdem*" was published in *Harvard Design Magazine* 16 (Winter–Spring 2002): 64–66.

The review of *Adolf Loos: A Private Portrait*, by Claire Beck Loos, edited by Carrie Paterson, was originally published in *West 86th: A Journal of Decorative Arts, Design History and Material Culture* 20, no. 1 (Spring–Summer 2013): 134–35.

The review of *Ich warne Sie vor Josef Hoffmann: Adolf Loos und die Wiener Werkstätte*, edited and written by Markus Kristan, was originally published in *West 86th: A Journal of Decorative Arts, Design History and Material* Culture 22, no. 2 (Fall–Winter 2015): 229–31.

Notes

Chapter 1

1| Ship manifests for 1893, Ellis Island Foundation, New York.

2| Burkhardt Rukschcio and Roland Schachel, *Adolf Loos: Leben und Werk.* 2nd ed. (Salzburg: Residenz, 1987), 20–21.

3| Roland L. Schachel describes this perfectly: "Loos' Leben ist zunächst die Emanzipationsgeschichte eines Sohnes aus kleinstädtischer Künstler- und Handwerkerschaft, die Geschichte eines verlorenen Sohnes, der bei seiner siegreichen Heimkunft weder erwartet noch gefeiert wurde, sondern den die Mutter hatte entmündigen lassen. Seine Entmündigung war die kleinbürgerliche Reaktion auf seinen erfolgreichen Versuch, aus den engen Grenzen seines Standes zu treten, um zu den Wurzeln des Menschentums zurückzukehren. Die endliche Wiedererlangung seiner Mündigkeit kann geradezu als Symbol für das Gelingen des Versuches angesehen werden, nach der Überwindung des Alten Menschen das eigene Selbst zu finden. In Amerika hat Loos die Niederungen menschlicher Existenz durchschritten und sich den Höheren Menschen selbst abgetrotz." Roland L. Schachel, "Aufgaben einer Loos-Biographie," in Burkhardt Rukschcio, ed., *Adolf Loos*, exhib. cat. (Vienna: Graphische Sammlung Albertina with the Historisches Museum der Stadt Wien, 1989), 17.

4| Dagmar Černoušková, Jindřich Chatrný, and Miroslava Menšiková, "Adolf Loos St., Brněnský sochár a kamenický mistr," in Jindřich Chatrný and Dagmar Černoušková, eds., *Brněnské stopy Adolfa Loose* (Brno: Muzeum města Brno, 2010), 7–17.

5| Claus Pack, "Adolf Loos (1870–1933)," in *Neue österreichische Biographie ab 1895* (Vienna: Amalthea, 1972), vol. 18, 132.

6| Rukschcio and Schachel, *Adolf Loos: Leben und Werk*, 20–21.

7| Ibid., 21.

8| Ibid.

9| Ship manifests for 1893, Ellis Island Foundation, New York; Rukschcio and Schachel, *Adolf Loos: Leben und Werk*, 21.

10| Rukschcio and Schachel, *Adolf Loos: Leben und Werk*, 21.

11| United States Federal Census, 1860; and Frederick Loos grave marker, Ivy Hill Cemetery, Philadelphia County, Pennsylvania. The gravestone records that Loos was born in Vienna on February 7, 1828 and died in Philadelphia on April 21, 1910. During the Civil War, he had served in the 13th Regiment of Missouri Volunteers, as a First Lieutenant, in Company A.

12| United States Federal Census, 1880. By the time young Adolf arrived, the family was living at 2141 Park Avenue in North Philadelphia. Philadelphia City Directories for 1893 and 1894.

13| Rukschcio and Schachel, *Adolf Loos: Leben und Werk*, 21.

14| Ibid.

15| How Loos was related to his uncle Benjamin is unclear. Loos never gives his surname or any other details. Further research would be required to establish the precise nature of their kinship.

16| Adolf Loos, *Das Andere: Ein Blatt zur Einführung abendländischer Kultur in Österreich* (1903), Nr. 1, 1; Rukschcio and Schachel, *Adolf Loos: Leben und Werk*, 22. Unless otherwise noted, all translations throughout this book are my own.

17| Ibid.

18| Eduard F. Sekler, "Josef Hoffmann, Adolf Loos und die Vereinigten Staaten" in Elisabeth Liskar, ed., *Wien und die Architektur des 20. Jahrhunderts* (Vienna: Böhlau, 1986), 127–28.

19| Ibid., 127.

20| Benedetto Gravagnuolo, *Adolf Loos: Theory and Work* (New York: Rizzoli, 1988), 49.

21| Schachel, "Aufgaben einer Loos-Biographie," 18.

22| Rukschcio and Schachel, *Adolf Loos: Leben und Werk*, 23–24.

23| Adolf Loos, "Der Silberhof und seine Nachbarschaft," *Neue Freie Presse*, 15 May 1898, 16.

24| Panayotis Tournikiotis, for example, offers a typical assessment: "Though he never met Adler or Sullivan, his memory was indelibly marked by the Chicago School, which existed simultaneously with the Greek revival that for half a century – since the end of the 1820s – had dominated monumental architecture in the United States." Panayotis Tournikiotis, *Adolf Loos* (New York: Princeton Architectural Press, 1994), 10.

25| Hermann Czech and Wolfgang Mistelbauer, *Das Looshaus*, 3rd ed. (Vienna: Löcker, 1984), 108.

26| Ludwig Münz, "Über die Grundlagen des Baustils von Adolf Loos," *Aufbau* 13 (1958): 393–95. Joseph Masheck made a similar argument in his later book. See Joseph Masheck, *Adolf Loos: The Art of Architecture* (London: I. B. Taurus, 2013), 151–53, 168.

27| Sekler, "Josef Hoffmann, Adolf Loos und die Vereinigten Staaten," 130.

28| Ibid.

29| Rukschcio and Schachel, *Adolf Loos: Leben und Werk*, 25.

30| Loos, *Das Andere,* Nr. 1, 1.

31| Rukschcio and Schachel, *Adolf Loos: Leben und Werk*, 25.

32| Ibid.

33| Richard Neutra, *Life and Shape* (New York: Appleton-Century-Crofts, 1962), 161.

34| Rukschcio and Schachel, *Adolf Loos: Leben und Werk*, 27.

35| Neutra, *Life and Shape*, 162–63.

36| Adolf Loos, "Möbel und Menschen," *Frankfurter Zeitung*, 28 May 1929, 3.

37| Rukschcio and Schachel, *Adolf Loos: Leben und Werk*, 27.

38| Adolf Loos, "Mein Aufreten mit der Melba," *Neues Wiener Tagblatt*, 20 January 1900, 1–3.

39| In the piece about Nellie Melba, Loos describes how he purportedly came to write criticism for the New York newspaper, but both the name of the paper, the *New York Bannerträger*, and the chief editor, John Smith, are clearly fictional. Ibid.

40| Rukschcio and Schachel, *Adolf Loos: Leben und Werk*, 29.

41| Ibid. See also Schachel, "Aufgaben einer Loos-Biographie," 23, 26, 29.

42| Neutra, *Life and Shape*, 161–62.

43| Ibid., 167.

44| Robert Scheu, "Adolf Loos," *Die Fackel*, 283/284 (26 June 1909): 31–32.

45| Sekler, "Josef Hoffmann, Adolf Loos und die Vereinigten Staaten," 130–31. What speaks strongly against the influence of Greenough is that he was all but forgotten in the 1890s; his rediscovery in America would come only fifty years later, in the 1940s. See the introduction in Harold A. Small, ed., *Horatio Greenough – Form and Function: Remarks on Art* (Berkeley: University of California Press, 1947). How much of his work or Sullivan's Loos might have been able to read is an open question, given that Loos's English was seemingly not up to understanding complex aesthetic arguments and many of Sullivan's seminal writings only appeared later. Sekler also ponders whether Loos might have been influenced by Henry David Thoreau, whose writings were available in German translation, but the likelihood is probably also small. More recently, Joseph Masheck has discussed a possible influence of Greenough's ideas on Loos, without adding any compelling evidence to the argument. See Masheck, *Adolf Loos: The Art of Architecture*, 109–10, 151–54.

46| Schachel, "Aufgaben einer Loos-Biographie," 18.

47| Ibid., 23.

48| Rukschcio and Schachel, *Adolf Loos: Leben und Werk*, 32.

49| Schachel, "Aufgaben einer Loos-Biographie," 26.

50| Adolf Loos, "Schulausstellung der Kunstgewerbeschule (Unsere Kunstgewerbeschule)," *Die Zeit* (Vienna), 31 October 1897.

51| Ibid.

52| Adolf Loos, "Weihnachtsausstellung im Österreichischen Museum," *Die Zeit,* 18 December 1897.

53| Adolf Loos, "Myrbach-Ausstellung," *Die Wage*, 2 April 1898; "Das Plakat der Kaiser-Jubiläumsausstellung," *Die Wage*, 2 April 1898; "Der Fall Scala," *Die Zeit*, 9 April 1898.

54| Adolf Loos, "Die Ausstellungsstadt: Der neue Stil," *Neue Freie Presse*, 8 May 1898, 16.

55| Ibid.

56| Loos, "Der Silberhof und seine Nachbarschaft," 16.

57| Ibid.

58| Ibid.

59| Ibid.

60| Paul Engelmann, *Letters from Ludwig Wittgenstein, with a Memoir* (Oxford: Blackwell, 1967), 131.

61| Ibid. 128.

62| Adolf Loos, "Der neue Stil und die Bronze-Industrie," *Neue Freie Presse*, 29 May 1898, 18.

63| Ibid.

64| Ibid.

65| In his review of the Kunstgewerbeschule exhibition, Loos writes, for example, while attacking with his usual fervor the problem of academic education: "In our land, people still believe that before a man can be entrusted with the design of a chair, he must know the five orders of Greek columns inside out. I think first and foremost he should know something about sitting!" Loos, "Schulausstellung der Kunstgewerbeschule (Unsere Kunstgewerbeschule)."

66| Adolf Loos, "Intérieurs: Ein Präludium," *Neue Freie Presse*, 5 June 1898, 16.

67| Ibid.

68| Adolf Loos, "Die Intérieurs in der Rotunde," *Neue Freie Presse*, 12 June 1898, 16.

69| Ibid.

70| Adolf Loos, "Das Luxusfuhrwerk," *Neue Freie Presse*, 3 July 1898, 16.

71| See Christopher Long, "The Origins and Context of Adolf Loos's 'Ornament and Crime,'" *Journal of the Society of Architectural Historians* 68, no. 2 (June 2009): 200–23, and reproduced in this book in chapter 2.

72| Adolf Loos, "Damenmode," first published 31 August 1898 in an unknown source; reprinted in *Dokumente der Frauen*, 1 March 1902.

73| Adolf Loos, "Die Schuhmacher," *Neue Freie Presse*, 14 August 1898, 7.

1| Carter Wiseman, "Adolf Loos," in Adolf K. Placek, ed., *Macmillan Encyclopedia of Architecture* (London: Macmillan, 1982), 3:31.

2| Ronnie M. Peplow, for example, argues that Loos "shocked the Viennese public in 1908": "Mit diesem Vortrag schockierte Adolf Loos 1908 das Wiener Publikum." "Adolf Loos: Die Verwerfung des wilden Ornaments," in Ursula Franke and Heinz Paetzold, eds., *Ornament und Geschichte: Studien zum Strukturwandel des Ornaments in der Moderne* (Bonn: Bouvier, 1996), 176. Mark Anderson writes: "An important document in the modernist rejection of the Jugendstil ... is Adolf Loos's polemical manifesto, 'Ornament and Crime,' first published in the *Neue Freie Presse* in 1908." Anderson, "The Ornaments of Writing: Kafka, Loos and the Jugendstil," *New German Critique* 43 (Winter 1988), 133. One early account placed the date of composition in the year 1907. See "Loos, Adolf," in *Wasmuths Lexikon der Baukunst*, vol. 3., ed. Leo Adler (Berlin, 1931), 546. Reyner Banham, writing in the late 1950s, added another element to the myth. He reported that the essay "had earned enough notice outside Vienna to earn republication ... in Herwarth Walden's Expressionist magazine, *der Sturm* [*sic*], in 1912" – apparently without checking the citation. (Loos, in fact, never published the essay in Walden's magazine.) Banham, "Ornament and Crime: The Decisive Contribution of Adolf Loos," *Architectural Review* 121 (February 1957): 88.

3| In his book *The Evolution of Allure*, George L. Hersey writes: "In 1908 Loos wrote an essay called "Ornament and Crime. ... It condemned all architectural ornament as atavistic." Hersey, *The Evolution of Allure: Sexual Selection from the Medici Venus to the Incredible Hulk* (Cambridge and London: MIT Press, 1996), 131.

4| Bernie Miller and Melody Ward, introduction, *Crime and Ornament: The Arts and Popular Culture in the Shadow of Adolf Loos*, ed. Bernie Miller and Melody Ward (Toronto: YYZ Books, 2002), 19.

5| Burkhardt Rukschcio, "Ornament und Mythos," in *Ornament und Askese im Zeitgeist des Wien der Jahrhundertwende*, ed. Alfred Pfabigan (Vienna: Brandstätter, 1985), 57–92.

6| Ibid., 58–61.

7| For an excellent chronology of the building's history, see Karlheinz Gruber, Sabine Höller-Alber, and Markus Kristan, *Ernst Epstein, 1881–1938: Der Bauleiter des Looshauses als Architekt* (Vienna: Holzhausen, 2002), 17–37.

8| "Der 'Kornspeicher' am Michaelerplatz," *Neuigkeits-Welt-Blatt*, 1 October 1910, 1.

9| "Wiener Bausorgen," *Berliner Lokal-Anzeiger*, 9 October 1910 (2nd suppl.), 6. Leslie Topp, citing this article, first noted the potential this reference might have for understanding the genesis of "Ornament and Crime." See Leslie Topp, *Architecture and Truth in Fin-de-Siècle Vienna* (Cambridge: Cambridge University Press, 2004), 207–8.

10| On Cassirer and his role in promoting the cause of modernism in Berlin, see Christian Kennert, *Paul Cassirer und sein Kreis: Ein Berliner Wegbereiter der Moderne* (Frankfurt am Main: Lang, 1996); Friedrich Pfaefflin, "Herwarth Walden und Karl Kraus, Adolf Loos, und Oskar Kokoschka: Die Anfänge im Kunstsalon Paul Cassirer – 1910," in R. Feilchenfeldt and T. Raff, eds., *Ein Fest der Kunste – Paul Cassirer: Der Kunsthändler als Verleger* (Munich: Beck, 2006).

11| On Walden and his place in the Berlin modern movement, see Freya Mulhaupt, ed., *Herwarth Walden, 1878–1941: Wegbereiter der Moderne* (Berlin: Berlinische Galerie, 1991); Nell Walden and Lothar Schreyer, eds., *Der Sturm – Ein Erinnerungsbuch an Herwarth Walden und die Kunstler aus dem Sturmkreis* (Baden-Baden: Klein, 1954).

12| On Kraus and his relationship with Loos in this period, see e.g., Edward Timms, *Karl Kraus – Apocalyptic Satirist: Culture and Catastrophe in Habsburg Vienna* (New Haven and London: Yale University Press, 1986), 6–9, 117–28.

13| George C. Avery, "Nachwort," in George C. Avery, ed., *Feinde in Scharen. Ein wahres Vergnugen dazusein – Karl Kraus-Herwarth Walden Briefwechsel 1909–1912* (Göttingen: Wallstein, 2002), 615. On Kraus and Walden's relationship, see also Peter Sprengel and Gregor Streim, *Berliner und Wiener Moderne: Vermittlungen und Abgrenzungen in Literatur, Theater, Publizistik* (Vienna: Böhlau, 1998).

14| Walden met Cassirer in 1909 through the actress Tilla Durieux, who married Cassirer the following year. Anja Walter-Ris, "Die Geschichte der Galerie Nierendorf: Kunstleidenschaft im Dienst der Moderne, Berlin/New York 1920–1995," PhD dissertation, Freie Universität Berlin, 2003, 36. Durieux, who had studied acting in Vienna, was well connected in cultural circles in Vienna and Berlin and was also acquainted with Kraus and Loos. Tilla Durieux, *Eine Tur steht offen: Erinnerungen* (Berlin: Herbig, 1954), 32–74.

15| The text reads: "adresse verloren 11 november sehr angenehm gruss dank = loos." [lost address 11 november is quite fine greetings thanks = loos.] Telegram from Adolf Loos to Herwarth Walden 11 September 1909, Sturm-Archiv, Staatsbibliothek zu Berlin – Preußischerkulturbesitz, Handschriftensammlung.

16| "Ich ... hoffe in den nächsten Tagen den Titel fur meinen Vortrag einsenden zu können. Bisher habe ich: 'Kritik der sogenannten angewandten Kunst.' Wenn Sie nichts gegen diesen Bandwurm haben, so kann es bleiben." Loos, addendum to a letter from Karl Kraus to Herwarth Walden, 18 September 1909, in Avery, ed., *Feinde in Scharen*, 62.

17| Letter from Kraus to Walden, 6 November 1909, in Avery, ed., *Feinde in Scharen*, 89. Kraus writes: "Ich fahre mit Loos bis Dresden. Das heißt: er bleibt dort ein paar Stunden und bereitet sich auf den Vortrag vor." [I will travel with Loos as far as Dresden. Which is to say: he will remain there for a couple of hours and prepare for the talk.]

18| Avery, ed., *Feinde in Scharen*, 447.

19| "Kleine Mitteilungen," *Berliner Tageblatt und Handels-Zeitung* 38 (11 November 1909); "Verein fur Kunst," *Vossische Zeitung* 6. Beilage (11 November 1909) (morning edition).

20| Just a year before, the critic Richard Schaukal described Loos as "an architect without buildings to build, an eloquent teacher lacking students, an enthusiastic fighter whose opponents on their daily journeys give him wide berth." Richard Schaukal, "Adolf Loos: Geistige Landschaft mit vereinzelter Figur im Vordergrund," *Innen-Dekoration* 19 (August 1908): 256. On the reception of Loos's work and ideas around this time, see Ludwig Hevesi, "Eine American Bar," *Kunst und Kunsthandwerk* 12 (1909): 214–15.

21| "Über 'Kritik der angewandten Kunst' sprach gestern abend Adolf Loos, ein in Wien bekannter Architekt und kunstgewerblicher Schriftsteller im Verein fur Kunst. Ein literarischer Schuler Peter Altenbergs, mit dem zusammen er vor Jahren auch eine kurzlebige Zeitschrift herausgab, sprach er Wienerisch fesselnd, nicht systhematische Theorien entwickelnd; er erzählte Geschichtchen mit zugespitzter Tendenz und gab dazwischen einige Apercus. Loos wendet sich mit großer Schärfe gegen den modernen Ruf nach kunstlerischer Ausgestaltung der Gebrauchsgegenstände. Kunst und Handwerk sollen voneinander geschieden werden; jene leite diese von ihrem eigentlichen Wesen ab, diese aber stehe unter keinem Schönheitsgesetz, sie solle nur dem Zweckgesetz gehorchen. So kommt Loos zu dem Satz, der den Grundgehalt seiner Ideen ausmacht: Evolutionen der Kultur sind gleichbedeutend mit der Entfernung der Ornamente aus den Gebrauchsgegenständen. Gewiß ist das ein guter Grundsatz als Gegengewicht gegen die Überästhetisierung der gewerblichen Erzeugnisse, als Ruckkehr zu ihrer Zweckbestimmung. Aus dieser erwächst fur Loos von selbst der jeweilige Stil, nach ihm die notwendige Einheit von Kultur und Kulturformen. Ja, aber besteht diese Einheit nicht auch heute, entsprechen nicht alle kunstgewerblichen Erzeugnisse unserer heutigen kulturellen Richtung? Also liegt in dieser der Fehler? In offenbaren Widerspruch stellt sich Loos, wenn er neben seinen Stilgedanken den Ruf nach Individualität stellt. Jeder richtet sich seine Wohnung nach dem individuellen Geschmack ein, heißt der eine Satz, den Loos aufstellt. Wie der Schneider heute einen Frack nach einer bestimmten Norm anfertigt, so solle man auch Möbel nur nach einem einheitlichen Muster anfertigen, sagt der andere Satz. Wo aber bleibt dabei die Individualität? Positives uber eine Einrichtung nach seinen Ideen, deren er in Wien einige ausgefuhrt hat, gab Loos leider nicht. Ihrer allgemeinen Tendenz wegen verdienen diese Ausfuhrungen Beachtung. Doch ist zu bemerken: wahre Kunst ist stets auch höchste Einfachheit und höchste Zweckmäßigkeit gewesen. Und das hat man doch in neuerer Zeit auch schon im Kunstgewerbe erkannt." *Berliner Börsen-Courier*, 12 November 1909 (1st suppl.), 7.

22| "Kritik der angewandten Kunst – das Wort 'Kunst' ist in Anfuhrungszeichen zu denken – war das Thema eines Vortrages, den gestern abend der Wiener Adolf Loos auf Veranlassung des Vereins fur Kunst im Salon Cassirer hielt. Eigentlich war es mehr eine Causerie, die durch größere Verbindlichkeit in der Form, ein weniger uberlegenes Niedersprechen des Gegners entschieden noch gewonnen hätte. Adolf Loos ist schon vor Jahren in seiner Heimat als Anreger von Gedanken fruchtbar gewesen, die heute erst modern zu werden beginnen. Er will die Emanzipation des Handwerks, er will dieses 'seinen naturlichen Instinkten uberlassen, die sich in Jahrhunderten bewährt haben.' Mit Luft und großer Energie wendet er sich gegen die Einmischung der Kunstler in rein praktische und private Angelegenheiten und bekämpft mit besonderer Schärfe Reformer wie Riemerschmidt [*sic*] und van der Velde. Das Verschwinden des Ornaments aus den täglichen Gebrauchsgegenständen, namentlich den Möbeln, gilt ihm als ein Ziel und Zeichen äußerer Kultur. In den Ausfuhrungen des Redners war ohne Zweifel viel Richtiges und Gesundes, trotz der ubertriebenen Bewunderung alles Englischen und eines wiederholten Vermengens der Begriffe 'Kultur' und 'Zivilisation.' An die Vorlesung schloß sich eine Art Frage- und Antwortspiel, das mancherlei Interessantes zutage förderte und dem Redner neben freundlichem Beifall auch einigen Widerspruch eintrug." *Berliner Lokal-Anzeiger*, 12 November 1909 (morning edition).

23| *Berliner Lokal-Anzeiger*, 12 November 1909 (morning edition); *Berliner Börsen-Courier*, 12 November 1909 (1st suppl.), 7.

24| The line in the original reads: "Ich habe folgende erkenntnis gefunden und der welt geschenkt: *evolution der kultur ist gleichbedeutend mit dem entfernen des ornamentes aus dem gebrauchsgegenstande* (emphasis in the original)." Loos, "Ornament und Verbrechen," in Adolf Loos, *Trotzdem 1900–1930* (Innsbruck: Brenner, 1931), 82.

25| "Architekt Loos ist bei uns durch seinen vorjährigen Vortrag: Ornament und Verbrechen, der so viel Wiederspruch erregte, bekannt geworden." Letter from Loos to Walden, Sturm-Archiv, Staatsbibliothek zu Berlin – Preußischerkulturbesitz, Handschriftensammlung. The letter is not dated, but it must have been written in September or early October 1910. The lecture took place on December 8, 1910.

26| "Wiener Bausorgen," *Berliner Lokal-Anzeiger*, 9 October 1910 (2nd suppl.), 6.

27| *Berliner Börsen-Courier*, 12 November 1909 (1st suppl.), 7 (see n. 21).

28| *Berliner Lokal-Anzeiger*, 12 November 1909 (morning edition).

29| "Der Titel muss nämlich so sein, dass die angewandten Kunstler reinkommen." Loos, addendum to a letter from Karl Kraus to Herwarth Walden, 18 September 1909, in Avery, ed., *Feinde in Scharen*, 62.

30| Undated letter from Loos to Walden, Sturm-Archiv (see n. 25).

31| Claire Loos, *Adolf Loos Privat* (Vienna: Böhlau, 1936), 105. Loos is often said to have had four wives, Lina Loss (born Carolina Catharina Obertimpfler), Bessie Bruce (born Elizabeth Bruce), Elsie Altmann-Loos, and Claire Beck Loos. He was never legally married to Bessie, however, because in Catholic Austria before 1918 one could not remarry without an annulment from the church. Loos, however, at times represented Bessie as his wife.

32| See Janet Stewart, *Fashioning Vienna: Adolf Loos's Cultural Criticism* (London and New York: Routledge, 2000), 22.

33| See, for example, Mitchell Schwarzer, "Ethnologies of the Primitive in Adolf Loos's Writings on Ornament," *Nineteenth-Century Contexts* 18 (1994), 225–47; Janet Stewart, "Talking of Modernity: The Viennese 'Vortrag' as Form," *German Life and Letters* 51 (October 1998), 455–70.

34| Adolf Loos, "Die Überflussigen," *März* 2, no. 3 (1908): 186.

35| See, for example, Karl Kraus, "Tagebuch," *Die Fackel* 11, nos. 279–80 (13 May 1909): 8. Scheu writes: "Die blankeiserne Schönheit der angelsächsischen Industrie, die glatte Fläche wird sein Idol und das Ornament sinkt ihm hinab zur 'Tätowierung.' Sein Lebensgedanke steigt herauf: Überwindung des Ornaments! Je weiter wir in der Kultur vorwärts schreiten, desto mehr befreien wir uns vom Ornament. Goldene Tressen sind heute noch ein Attribut der Hörigkeit. Das Bedurfnis zu ornamentieren durchschaut er als Indianerstandpunkt." Robert Scheu, "Adolf Loos," *Die Fackel* 11, nos. 283–84 (26 June 1909): 32–33. See also the articles by Wilhelm von Wymetal, "Ein reichbegabtes Brunner Kind (Adolf Loos 'Architekt und Schriftsteller, Kunstler und Denker')," originally published in *Tagesbote aus Mähren und Schlesien*, 4 January 1908; reprinted in *Konfrontationen:*

Schriften von und uber Adolf Loos, ed. Adolf Opel (Vienna: Prachner, 1988), 21–31; Ludwig Hevesi, "Gegen das moderne Ornament: Adolf Loos," *Fremden-Blatt*, 22 November 1907, 15–16.

36| Adolf Loos, "Das Luxusfuhrwerk," *Neue Freie Presse*, 3 July 1898, 16; reprinted in Adolf Loos, *Ins Leere gesprochen* (Paris: George Crès, 1921), 70–75.

37| For a discussion of Loos's early writings, see Hildegund Amanhauser, *Untersuchungen zu den Schriften von Adolf Loos* (Vienna, VWGÖ 1985); Debra Schafter, *The Order of Ornament, The Structure of Style: Theoretical Foundations of Modern Art and Architecture* (Cambridge: Cambridge University Press, 2003), 185–90, 193–94; Mitchell Schwarzer, *German Architectural Theory and the Search for Modern Identity* (Cambridge: Cambridge University Press, 1995), esp. 238–47.

38| Burkhardt Rukschcio and Roland Schachel, *Adolf Loos: Leben und Werk* (Salzburg: Residenz, 1982), 114–15, 118.

39| Loos, "Die Überflussigen (Deutscher Werkbund)," *März: Halbmonatsschrift der deutsche Kultur* 2, no. 3 (1908): 185–87; Loos, "Lob der Gegenwart," *März: Halbmonatsschrift der deutsche Kultur* 2, no. 3 (1908): 310–12; Loos, "Kultur," *März: Halbmonatsschrift der deutsche Kultur* 2, no. 4 (1908): 134–36.

40| Adolf Loos, *Trotzdem 1900–1930* (Innsbruck: Brenner, 1931).

41| Gregor Streim, "Vienna–Berlin Circa 1910: Avant-Garde and Metropolitan Culture," in *Oskar Kokoschka: Early Portraits from Vienna and Berlin, 1909–1914*, ed. Tobias G. Natter (New Haven and London: Yale University Press, 2002), 22; Werner J. Schweiger, *Der junge Kokoschka: Leben und Werk, 1904–1914* (Vienna and Munich: Brandstätter, 1983), 209–34.

42| Oskar Maurus Fontana, "Expressionismus in Wien, Erinnerungen," in Paul Raabe, ed., *Expressionismus: Aufzeichnungen und Erinnerungen der Zeitgenossen* (Freiburg: Walter, 1965), 189.

43| Streim, "Vienna–Berlin Circa 1910," 22.

44| "Ornament und Verbrechen," *Fremden-Blatt*, 22 January 1910, 21.

45| Ibid.

46| See Adolf Loos, *Wohnungswanderungen* (Vienna, 1907).

47| Loos was a regular at the Café Museum on Karlsplatz, a short distance from the two schools. Students often sat at his table and listened to him talk about his views on architecture and design. See Loos's own description of his "school," "Meine Bauschule," in *Trotzdem*, 64–67.

48| "Ornament und Verbrechen," *Fremden-Blatt*, 22 January 1910, 21.

49| Letter from Kraus to Walden, 22 December 1909, in Avery, ed., *Feinde in Scharen*, 129–30.

50| Telegram from Loos and Kraus to Walden, in Avery, ed., *Feinde in Scharen*, 140; postcard from Kraus to Walden, in ibid., 145. Loos, who had met Kokoschka the previous year, took the young artist under his wing and sought to find him commissions and exhibition opportunities. Oskar Kokoschka, *My Life*, trans. David Britt (New York: Macmillan, 1974), 49.

51| Rukschcio and Schachel, *Adolf Loos*, 147.

52| Robert Oerley, "Jahresbilanz," in *Jahrbuch der Gesellschaft österreichischer Architekten*

1909–1910 (Vienna, 1910), 101. Oerley, an important modernist architect in his own right, was a friend of Loos's. Andrew Barker and Leo A. Lensing, *Peter Altenberg: Rezept die Welt zu sehen* (Vienna: Braumuller, 1995), 416.

53| Richard von Schaukal, untitled essay in *Adolf Loos zum 60. Geburtstag am 10. Dezember 1930* (Vienna: Lanyi, 1930), 46.

54| Rukschcio, "Ornament und Mythos," 61.

55| Loos, manuscript for "Ornament und Verbrechen," [1910], 9; private collection.

56| Franz Gluck, ed., *Adolf Loos: Sämtliche Schriften in zwei Bänden* (Vienna: Herold, 1962), vol. 1. Only the first volume was published; the second volume never appeared.

57| Loos, "Ornament und Verbrechen," *Frankfurter Zeitung*, 24 October 1929.

58| Gluck, "Nachwort des Herausgebers," in Gluck, ed., *Adolf Loos: Sämtliche Schriften*, 1:466.

59| Loos, "Ornament und Verbrechen," *Frankfurter Zeitung*, 24 October 1929.

60| See, for example, Carma Gorman, ed., *The Industrial Design Reader* (New York: Allworth, 2003), 74–81.

61| Rukschcio, "Ornament und Mythos," 61.

62| Loos writes: "The ornament that is being created today bears no connection with us… . It has no potential for present-day development. Where is Otto Eckmann's ornament now … ?" Loos, "Ornament und Verbrechen," in *Trotzdem*, 88–89.

63| See, for example, Anderson, "The Ornaments of Writing," 134–35. In "Cultural Degeneration," however, Loos acknowledges that although Hoffmann had dispensed with "fretwork since the Café Museum, and, as far as constructional techniques are concerned, has come closer to my own manner. But even today he can improve the appearance of his furniture with peculiar stains, with stencils and inlaid decoration." Loos, "Kulturentartung," in *Trotzdem*, 79.

64| Loos, "Ein Wiener Architckt," *Dekorative Kunst* 1 (1898), 227.

65| Josef Hoffmann, "Einfache Möbel: Entwurfe und begleitende Worte von Professor Josef Hoffmann," *Das Interieur* 2 (1901), 37. On the growing mutual antipathy between Loos and Hoffmann, see Rainald Franz, "Josef Hoffmann and Adolf Loos: The Ornament Controversy in Vienna," in *Josef Hoffmann Designs*, ed. Peter Noever, exhib. cat. (Munich: Prestel, 1992), 12–13.

66| Loos, "Wohnungsmoden," *Frankfurter Zeitung*, 8 December 1907, 1; Franz, "Josef Hoffmann and Adolf Loos," 14.

67| Loos, "Die Überflussigen," 187.

68| "Kritik der angewandten Kunst," *Berliner Lokal-Anzeiger*, 12 November 1909.

69| Loos, "Ornament und Verbrechen," in *Trotzdem*, 82. See also Werner Hoffmann, "Das Fleisch erkennen," in Alfred Pfabigan, ed., *Ornament und Askese im Zeitgeist des Wien der Jahrhundertwende* (Vienna: Brandstätter, 1985), 120–21, 128.

70| Albert Ehrenstein, "Vom Gehen, Stehen, Sitzen, Liegen, Schlafen, Essen, Trinken," *Berliner Tageblatt*, 28 November 1911.

71| Cesare Lombroso, *L'uomo delinquente* (Milan: Hoepli, 1876). See also Lombroso's related discussion in *Palimsesti dal carcere: Raccolta unicamente destinata ogli uomini di scienza* (Turin: Fratelli Broca, 1888). Among the many scholars who have suggested Lombroso as the source of Loos's ideas of criminality and ornament, see, e.g., Mark Anderson, *Kafka's Clothes: Ornament and Aestheticism in the Habsburg Fin de Siècle* (New York and Oxford: Oxford University Press, 1995), 180–82; Jimena Canales and Andrew Herscher, "Criminal Skins: Tattoos and Modern Architecture in the Work of Adolf Loos," *Architectural History* 48 (2005), 235–56; George L. Hersey, *The Evolution of Allure*, 131; Sherwin Simmons, "Ornament, Gender, and Interiority in Viennese Expressionism," *Modernism/Modernity* 8, no. 2 (April 2001), 245–76.

72| [72] Cesare Lombroso, *Der Verbrecher, in anthropologischer, ärztlicher und juristischer Beziehung*, trans. O. M. Fraenkel, 2 vols. (Hamburg: Richter, 1887), 254.

73| Ibid.

74| Ákos Moravánszky contends that Loos "took over" Lombroso's sentences on tattooing and criminality "from *L'uomo deliquente* [*sic*] almost unchanged." Ákos Moravánszky, *Competing Visions: Aesthetic Invention and Social Imagination in Central European Architecture, 1867–1918* (Cambridge and London: MIT Press, 1998), 370. Stephan Oettermann, *Zeichen auf der Haut: Die Geschichte der Tätowierung in Europa* (Frankfurt am Main: Syndikat, 1979), 64, makes a similar argument. Lombroso does describe the practice of tattooing in Polynesia in *L'uomo delinquente*, but there is little else in his discussion, aside from his notion that tattooing is linked with modern criminality, that is directly reproduced in Loos's text.

75| Owen Jones, *The Grammar of Ornament* (London: Day and Son, 1856), frontis. ff. See also Hubert Damisch, "L'Autre 'Ich,' L'Autriche-Austria, or the Desire for the Void: Toward a Tomb for Adolf Loos," *Grey Room* 1 (2000), 33, 40.

76| Loos, "Ornament und Verbrechen," in *Trotzdem*, 82.

77| On Andreas Reischek's expedition, see his book, *Sterbende Welt: Zwölf Jahre Forscherleben auf Neuseeland* (Leipzig: Brockhaus, 1924).

78| Rudolf Pöch, *Zweiter Bericht über meine phonographischen Aufnahmen in Neu-Guinea (Britisch-Neu-Guinea vom 7. Oktober bis zum 1. Februar 1906)* (Vienna: Alfred Hölder, 1907). See also Canales and Herscher, "Criminal Skins," 253. In his earliest writing on the ornament problem, "Das Luxusfuhrwerk," Loos had used the imagery not of the primitive Papuan, but the "Indianer," and he refers to the reliance on ornament as an "Indianerstandpunkt" – an "Indian attitude." Only later, perhaps in response to Pöch's research, did he begin using the "Papuaner." Loos, "Das Luxusfuhrwerk," in Loos, *Ins Leere gesprochen*, 72, 75.

79| Gina Lombroso-Ferrero, *Criminal Man According to the Classification of Cesare Lombroso* (New York and London: Putnam, 1911; 1972), 134.

80| Loos, "Ornament und Verbrechen," in *Trotzdem*, 81.

81| Max Nordau, *Entartung*, 2 vols. (Berlin: C. Duncker, 1893).

82| Max Nordau, *Menschen und Menschliches von heute* (Berlin: Vereins der Bucherfreunde, 1915), 30.

83| Nordau, preface to *Entartung*, translated as *Degeneration* (New York: Appleton, 1895); rpt. (Lincoln, Nebraska: University of Nebraska Press, 1993), v.

84| See George L. Mosse, introduction," Nordau, *Degeneration*, esp. xiii–xx.
85| Loos, "Ornament und Verbrechen," in *Trotzdem*, 82.
86| Mosse, introduction, xvii.
87| Loos, "Ornament und Verbrechen," in *Trotzdem*, 93.
88| Gottfried Semper, *Der Stil in den technischen und tektonischen Kunste; oder Praktische Aesthetik. Ein Handbuch fur Techniker, Kunstler und Kunstfreunde,* 2 vols. (Frankfurt am Main: Verlag fur Kunst und Wissenschaft, 1860–63).
89| Alois Reigl, *Stilfragen: Grundlegungen zu einer Geschichte der Ornamentik* (Berlin: Georg Siemens, 1893).
90| Jan Zwicky, for example, has attacked Loos for his alleged "racist" and "sociobiological" comments, contending that his argument is "imbued with progress mythology" and "sentiment about class hierarchies." Zwicky, "Integrity and Ornament," in Miller and Ward, eds., *Crime and Ornament*, 205.
91| "Der menschliche embryo macht im mutterleibe alle entwicklungsphasen des tierreiches durch." Loos, "Ornament und Verbrechen," in *Trotzdem*, 81.
92| See Ernst Haeckel, *Die Welträtsel: Gemeinverständliche Studien uber monistische Philosophie* (Leipzig: Kröner, 1899).
93| Ernst Haeckel, *Kunstformen der Natur* (Leipzig: Bibliographischen Instituts, 1899–1903).
94| See, e.g., Jörg Mathes, *Theorie des literarischen Jugendstils* (Stuttgart: Reclam, 1984), 32.
95| Banham, "Ornament and Crime," 86.
96| See Rukschcio, "Ornament und Mythos," 58.
97| Ibid., 59. On the larger ornament debate in Germany, see María Ocón Fernández, *Ornament und Moderne: Theoriebildung und Ornamentdebatte im deutschen Architekturdiskurs (1850–1930)* (Berlin: Reimer, 2004); Gérard Raulet and Burghart Schmidt, eds., *Kritische Theorie des Ornaments* (Vienna: Böhlau, 1993).
98| Joseph August Lux, "Die Erneuerung der Ornamentik," *Innen-Dekoration* 18 (1907): 291.
99| Richard Schaukal, "Gegen das Ornament," *Deutsche Kunst und Dekoration* 22 (April 1908): 12–13, 15.
100| Schaukal writes: "Ein Tuchtiger hat schon vor Jahren den Kampf gegen das willkurliche Ornament aufgenommen: *Adolf Loos*, ein Wiener Architekt. Ihm ist die Lösung: 'Los vom Ornament!' eine Glaubens- und Gewissenssache. Er sieht in der ornamentlosen Zukunft, die er erträumt, die Menschheit von einem Fluch befreit, sieht nutzlose Arbeit abgetan, die Produktion vereinfacht, den Gewinn, zumal der Handwerker, mit geringern Mitteln erzielbar." Ibid.
101| Wilhelm Michel, "Die Schicksale des Ornaments," *Innen-Dekoration* 20 (1909): 232.
102| Otto Scheffers, "Zweckform und Ornament," *Deutsche Kunst und Dekoration* 24 (1909): 238.
103| Anton Jaumann, "Der moderne Mensch und das Kunstgewerbe," *Innen-Dekoration* 21 (January 1910): 1. See also Wilhelm Michel, "Neue Tendenzen in Kunstgewerbe," *Innen-Dekoration* 21 (1910): 127–28, 135; E. W. Bredt, "Kunstler und Helden," *Innen-Dekoration* 21 (July 1910): 290, 293–94.
104| Otto Schulze-Elberfeld, "Über Ornament-Symbolik," *Innen-Dekoration* 21 (1910): 378.
105| Georg Simmel, "Das Probem des Stiles," *Dekorative Kunst* 11 (April 1908): 310.

106| The essay, as Hélène Furján has observed, also engages the politics of ornament. See Furján, "Dressing Down: Adolf Loos and the Politics of Ornament," *Journal of Architecture* 8, no. 1 (2003): 115–30.

107| Hermann Muthesius, "Wirtschaftsformen im Kunstgewerbe," lecture presented to the Volkswirtschaftliche Gesellschaft in Berlin, 30 January 1908, quoted in Peter Haiko and Mara Reissberger, "Ornamentlosigkeit als neuer Zwang," in *Ornament und Askese im Zeitgeist des Wien der Jahrhundertwende*, ed. Alfred Pfabigan (Vienna: Brandstätter, 1985), 110–11.

108| The Dresden-based designer Karl Grosz, for example, argued in the 1912 annual of the German Werkbund that "Ornamental embellishment for objects for use by the broad public leads to a devaluation of their worth." Karl Grosz, "Das Ornament," *Jahrbuch des Deutschen Werkbundes 1912* (Jena: Diederichs, 1912), 63.

109| Loos, "Ornament und Verbrechen," in *Trotzdem*, 90–91.

110| Avery, ed., *Feinde in Scharen*, 148–69. Loos also arranged for Kokoschka to move to Berlin and take up a post as one of the editors of the journal. Dietrich Worbs, "Adolf Loos in Berlin," in Dietrich Worbs, ed., *Adolf Loos 1870–1933 Raumplan-Wohnungsbau*, exhib. cat. (Berlin: Akademie der Kunste, 1994), 7.

111| Loos, letter to Walden, 25 February 1910, Sturm-Archiv.

112| *Berliner Tageblatt*, 3 March 1910, 2nd suppl.

113| Unsigned and untitled review of "Ornament and Crime" in *Berliner Tageblatt*, 4 March 1910, 6th suppl.

114| Loos, "Ornament und Verbrechen," in *Trotzdem*, 81.

115| "Zwanzig Zuhörer klatschen ihm gestern Beifall," *Berliner Tageblatt*, 4 March 1910, 6th suppl. Among those in attendance were Kraus, Walden, Cassirer, and Lasker-Schuler.

116| "Der Ornamentfeind," *Der Ulk: Illustriertes Wochenblatt fur Humor und Satire, Beilage zum Berliner Tageblatt*, 11 (18 March 1910).

117| "Lieber Ulk! Und ich sage Dir, es wird die Zeit kommen, in der die Einrichtung einer Zelle vom Hoftapezierer Schulze oder Professor Van de Velde als Strafverschärfung gelten wird. Adolf Loos, "Ornament und Verbrechen," *Der Sturm* 1, no. 6 (7 April 1910): 44. The title of his piece, "Ornament und Verbrechen," has mislead some scholars into citing this as the first, or an early, publication of Loos's talk.

118| Adolf Loos, "Adolf Loos Architekt (Selbstdarstellung)," first published in *Meister-Archiv: Gallerie von Zeitgenossen Deutschlands* (Berlin: Eckstein, 1915), reprinted in Opel, ed., *Konfrontationen*, 83.

119| Rukschcio and Schachel, *Adolf Loos*, 148.

120| Loos, "Wiener Architekturfragen," *Reichspost*, 1 October 1910, 1–2; "Mein erstes Haus!," *Der Morgen*, 3 October 1910, 1.

121| Gruber et al., *Ernst Epstein*, 25.

122| Loos, postscript to a letter from Kraus to Walden, 17 November 1910, in Avery, ed., *Feinde in Scharen*, 275.

123| Loos, "Über Architektur," *Der Sturm* 1, no. 42 (15 December 1910): 334; Loos, "Architektur," in *Trotzdem*, 95–113. It is worth noting that "Architektur" as it appears in

Trotzdem is also misdated. The date assigned to the essay is 1909, although Loos almost certainly wrote the piece in November or early December 1910 as the controversy over the Michaelerplatz building was gathering momentum. Here again, the misdating evidently occurred when Kulka and Gluck were preparing *Trotzdem*. They apparently asked Loos, who must have misremembered the year of the talk.

124| Loos, "Architektur," in *Trotzdem*, 98.

125| On Loos's specific images of the "primitive" and vernacular design in the essay, see J. Duncan Derry, "Loos's Primitivism," *Midgård* 1, no. 1 (1987): 57–61.

126| Loos, "Architektur," in *Trotzdem*, 111–12.

127| Ibid., 112–13.

128| "Vom Neuen Verein," *Munchner Neueste Nachrichten*, 12 December 1910.

129| M. K. R., "Ornament und Verbrechen," *Munchner Neueste Nachrichten*, 17 December 1910.

130| "[Loos] gehört zu den interessantesten Charakterköpfen der Wiener Kunstlerwelt ... [er] vertritt, wenn man so sagen darf, den Radikalismus der Sachlichkeit, ein Prinzip, das er jetzt auch praktisch, an dem vielbesprochenen Neubau auf dem Wiener Michaelerplatz anschaulich gemacht hat." [Ludwig Steiner?], "Adolf Loos: Zu seinem heutigen Vortrag im deutsch-polytechnischen Verein," *Prager Tagblatt*, 17 March 1911, 7.

131| Vladimír Šlapeta, "Adolf Loos' Vorträge in Prag und Brunn," in Burkhardt Rukschcio, ed., *Adolf Loos*; exhib. cat. (Vienna: Graphische Sammlung Albertina, 1989), 41–42; Anderson, *Kafka's Clothes*, 181. See also Vladimír Šlapeta, "Adolf Loos a česká architektura," *Památky a příroda* 10 (1983), 596–602.

132| [Ludwig Steiner?], "Vortrag Adolf Loos," *Prager Tagblatt*, 18 March 1911, 9.

133| Ibid.

134| See, for example, Vladimír Šlapeta, "Adolf Loos und die tschechische Architektur," in *Wien und die Architektur des 20. Jahrhunderts: Akten des XXV. Internationalen Kongresses fur Kunstgeschichte, Wien 4.–10. Sept. 1983*, ed. Elisabeth Liskar (Vienna: Böhlau, 1986), 88–89.

135| Rukschcio and Schachel, *Adolf Loos*, 155. See also "Vom Gehen, Stehen, Sitzen, Liegen, Essen, und Trinken," *Illustriertes Wiener Extrablatt*, 25 March 1911, 8.

136| Adolf Loos, "Vom Gehen, Stehen, Sitzen, Liegen, Schlafen, Essen, Trinken," *Der Sturm* 2, no. 87 (November 1911), 691–92.

137| Walden, letter to Kraus, 15 August 1911, in Avery, ed., *Feinde in Scharen*, 348–49, 548.

138| Loos, "Mein Haus am Michaelerplatz," reprinted in *Parnass*, special issue, "Der Kunstlerkreis um Adolf Loos: Aufbruch zur Jahrhundertwende" (1985): ii–xv; Rukschcio and Schachel, *Adolf Loos*, 163.

139| "Das Haus am Michaelerplatz," *Wiener Mittags-Zeitung*, 12 December 1911, 2; "Das Loos-Haus auf dem Michaelerplatze," *Neue Freie Presse*, 12 December 1911, 7–8.

140| Gruber et al., *Ernst Epstein*, 32.

141| Rukschcio, "Ornament und Mythos," 58.

142| In his autobiographical sketch of 1915, Loos cites a newspaper review of the talk from the *Munchener Zeitung*: "R. B. Der Sinn seiner Ausfuhrungen ist in Kürze der: Ornament is Verbrechen am Geiste der Kunst, und die Kunst hat mit Architektur nichts zu tun (das

Grabmal und das Denkmal ausgenommen). Das klingt wie ein Paradoxon und ist auch ein solches. Und noch vieles Andere, was Loos in sehr zugespitzter, scharf pointierter Formulierung in den Saal schleudert, hörte sich paradox an, und Einzelnes schlug sogar wie eine Bombe ein."Adolf Loos Architekt (Selbstdarstellung)," reprinted in Opel, ed., *Konfrontationen*, 83. The reference here to Loos's ideas about architecture suggests that the talk was given in 1911, when he was combining elements of "Ornament and Crime" and "Über Architektur." There is also a passing reference to "Ornament and Crime" in the Munich-based cultural magazine *Der Zwiebelfisch*, "Vandalismus in Wien," *Der Zwiebelfisch* 3, no. 4 (1911), 140.

143| Thor Beenfeldt, "Adolf Loos," *Architekten: Meddelelser fra akademisk architektforening* (Copenhagen) 15, no. 27 (5 April 1913), 266–267. I would like to thank Jan Christer Eriksson and Kristina Wängberg-Eriksson for translating this article for me.

144| Loos, "Ornement et crime," Marcel Ray trans., *Les cahiers d'aujourd'hui* 5 (June 1913), 247–56.

145| In 1911, Loos had begun work on a design for a school building for Eugenie Schwarzwald in the resort community on the Semmering mountain, south of Vienna. The design was not realized, but a full set of drawings of the project survives. Rukschcio and Schachel, *Adolf Loos*, 178, 489–92.

146| Loos, "L'Architecture et le style moderne," trans. Marcel Ray, out *Les cahiers d'aujourd'hui* 2 (December 1912), 82–92.

147| Reyner Banham, *Theory and Design in the First Machine Age* (Cambridge: MIT Press, 1980), 89.

148| Loos, "Ornement et crime," 248. I would like to thank Natsumi Nonaka for pointing this out to me. I reproduced Loos's famous axiom here using his preferred orthography – i.e., not capitalizing most nouns expect those that are proper or begin a sentence, in contrast to standard German-language rules. Loos adopted this practice later in his writing career, but it was applied unevenly in his publications, depending on whether the editors or publishers of his works accepted the idea. Here, as elsewhere in this book, I have sometimes used Loos's own idiosyncratic versions. But careful readers will notice that in other instances – depending on how it was printed – I have quoted the renderings following the traditional spelling rules – just as they originally appeared.

149| Banham, *Theory and Design*, 89.

150| Le Corbusier read the French-language versions of "Ornament and Crime" and "Architecture" in *Les cahiers d'aujourd'hui* in the early fall of 1913. Auguste Perret lent the two issues to the young Corbusier, who mentions them in a letter to Perret in late November 1913. See Francesco Passanti, "Architecture: Proportion, Classicism and Other Issues," in *Le Corbusier before Le Corbusier: Applied Arts, Architecture, Painting, Photography, 1907–1922*, ed. Stanislaus von Moos and Arthur Ruegg, exhib. cat. (New Haven: Yale University Press, 2002), 89 and 292, note 97. Le Corbusier reprinted the essay as "Ornement et crime," in *L'Esprit nouveau* 2 (November 1920), 159–68; in his foreword, he writes: "Loos is one of the predecessors of the new spirit. Around 1900, when enthusiasm for the Jugendstil was at its apex, in the era of excessive décor, Loos began his crusade against these tendencies." Le Corbusier, *L'Esprit nouveau* 2 (November 1920), 159.

151| Loos, "Ornement et Crime," *L'Architecture vivante* 4 (Spring 1926), 28–30; "Ornament und Verbrechen," *Frankfurter Zeitung*, 24 October 1929.

152| Loos, "Ornament und Verbrechen," *Prager Tagblatt*, 10 November 1929, iv.

153| [Heinrich Kulka?], foreword to "Ornament und Verbrechen," *Prager Tagblatt*, 24 October 1929, iv. This foreword is also reprinted in Gluck, ed., *Adolf Loos*, 457–58.

154| Loos, "Ornament und Erziehung," in *Trotzdem*, 200–204.

Chapter 3

1| Adolf Loos, untitled article in *Das Andere: Ein Blatt zur Einführung abendländischer Kultur in Österreich* 1, no. 2 (15 October 1903): 2. See also Markus Kristan, ed., *Adolf Loos: Läden & Lokale* (Vienna: Album, 2001), 18–19.

2| See, for example, Stanford Anderson, "The Legacy of German Neoclassicism and Biedermeier: Behrens, Tessenow, Loos, and Mies," *Assemblage* 15 (August 1991): 63–87.

3| On the origins and course of the Biedermeier revival in Vienna, see Paul Asenbaum, Stefan Asenbaum, and Christian Witt-Dörring, eds., *Moderne Vergangenheit: Wien 1800–1900*, exhib. cat. (Vienna, 1981).

4| Ludwig Hevesi, "Biedermeier und Komp.," first published in *Fremden-Blatt*, 29 November 1901, reprinted in Ludwig Hevesi, *Altkunst-Neukunst: Wien 1894–1908* (Vienna: Konegan, 1909), 188.

5| Ibid., 190.

6| Ibid., 190–91.

7| Joseph August Lux, "Biedermeier als Erzieher," *Hohe Warte* 1 (1904–05), 145. On Lux and his role in modern architecture design in Vienna, see Mark Jarzombek, "Joseph August Lux: Werkbund Promoter, Historian of a Lost Modernity," *Journal of the Society of Architectural Historians* 63, no. 2 (June 2004): 202–19.

8| Julius Langbehn, *Rembrandt als Erzieher. Von einem Deutschen* (Leipzig: C. L. Hirschfeld, 1890).

9| Lux, "Biedermeier als Erzieher," 148.

10| Ibid., 149.

11| On Loos's views on the persistence of classicism, see, e.g., Ludwig Münz, "Die alte und die neue Richtung in der Baukunst von Adolf Loos," *Alte und Neue Kunst* 2, no. 3 (1953): 115–20.

12| Joseph Folnesics, ed., *Innenräume und Hausrat der Empire- und Biedermeierzeit in Österreich-Ungarn: Lichtdrucktafeln mit geschichtlich erläuterndem Text* (Vienna: Anton Schroll, 1903); Alois Riegl, "Möbel und Innendekoration des Empire" (1898); reprinted in Karl M. Swoboda, ed., *Alois Riegl: Gesammelte Aufsätzte* (Vienna: Dr. B. Filser, 1929), 10-27. See also, "Alte und neue Möbel," *Das Interieur* 4 (1903): 34; Hartwig Fischel, "Das Wiener Möbel von einst und jetzt," *Das Interieur* 1 (1900): 97–104; Ernst Wilhelm Bredt, "Bruno Paul – Biedermeier – Empire," *Dekorative Kunst* 8 (March 1905): 217–29.

13| Joseph August Lux, *Empire und Biedermeier: Eine Sammlung von Möbeln und Innenräumen* (Stuttgart: Julius Hoffmann, 1906).

14| Paul, Mebes ed., *Um 1800: Architektur und Handwerk im letzten Jahrhundert ihrer traditionellen Entwicklung*, 2 vols. (Munich: F. Bruckmann, 1908).

15| Ibid., vol. 1., 19–20.

16| Ibid., vol. 1., 21–22.

17| Josef Hoffmann, "Einfache Möbel," *Das Interieur* 2 (1901): 37.

18| On Hoffmann's turn to classicism, see Eduard F. Sekler, *Josef Hoffmann: Das architektonische Werk* (Salzburg: Residenz, 1982), 101–64.

19| Christopher Long, *Josef Frank: Life and Work* (Chicago: University of Chicago Press, 2002), 19–27.

20| See, for example, Hans Tietze, "Der Kampf um Alt-Wien: III. Wiener Neubauten," *Kunstgeschichtliches Jahrbuch der k.k. Zentral-Kommission für Erforschung und Erhaltung der Kunst- und Historischen Denkmale* 4, Beiblatt (1910): 33–63.

21| On Loos's ideas of cultural context, see Stanford Anderson, "Architecture in a Cultural Field," in Taisto Mäkela and Wallis Miller, eds., *Wars of Classification: Architecture and Modernity* (New York: Princeton Architectural Press, 1991), 9–35.

22| Adolf Loos, "Architektur," written in 1910, republished in Adolf Loos, *Trotzdem 1900–1930* (Innsbruck: Brenner, 1931), 105–06.

23| Adolf Loos, "Ein Wiener Architekt," *Dekorative Kunst* 2 (1898): 227.

24| On the problem of originality for Loos, see, for example, Hubert Locher, "'Geung der originalgenies! Wiederholen wir uns unaufhörlich selbst!' Adolf Loos, das Neue und 'Das Andere,'" *Daidalos* 52 (15 June 1994): 76–85.

25| Loos, "Architektur," 104.

26| Ibid.

27| Ibid., 106.

28| Locher, "'Genung der originalgenies!,'" 79. See also Loos's pamphlet *Wohnungswanderungen* (Vienna, 1907), in which he summarizes his ideas on craft and ornament.

29| Adolf Loos, "Der neue Stil und die Wiener Bronze-Industrie," *Neue Freie Presse*, 29 May 1898, 16.

30| Ibid.

31| See Locher, "'Genung der originalgenies!,'" 84.

32| Loos, "Architektur," 106–07.

33| Adolf Loos, "Möbel," *Neue Freie Presse*, 2 October 1898, 16.

34| Ibid., 120–21

35| See Loos's article "Josef Veillich" (1929), in Loos, *Trotzdem*, 246–53.

36| Locher, "'Genung der originalgenies!,'" 79.

37| Loos, "Der neue Stil und die Wiener Bronze-Industrie," 16.

Chapter 4

1| Adolf Loos, *Trotzdem 1900–1930* (Innsbruck: Brenner, 1931), 5.

2| Adolf Loos, *Ins Leere gesprochen*, 1897–1900 (Paris and Zurich: Georges Crés, 1921).

3| The second edition of the book, published the same year, contains two additional essays, "Der Staat und die Kunst" (The State and Art) and "Oskar Kokoschka." The former is a shortened version of the foreword to Loos's essay in *Richtlinien für ein Kunstamt*, published in Vienna by Richard Lanyi in 1919. The essay on Kokoschka, which Loos wrote about an exhibition of his friend's work at the Kunsthalle in Mannheim, was not published until January 1931, when the first edition was already in press.

4| Adolf Loos, *Spoken into the Void: Collected Essays 1897–1900*, intro. Aldo Rossi, trans. Jane O. Newman and John H. Smith (Cambridge: MIT Press, 1982); Adolf Loos, *Ornament and Crime: Selected Essays*, ed. Adolf Opel, trans. Michael Mitchell (Riverside, California: Ariadne Press, 1998).

5| Otto Stoessl, "Erinnerung an Adolf Loos," *Welt im Wort* (Vienna), 7 December 1933, reprinted in Opel, ed., *Konfrontationen: Schriften von und uber Adolf Loos*, ed. Adolf Opel (Vienna: Prachner, 1988), 167.

6| Brenner Verlag was owned and operated by Loos's friend, Ludwig von Ficker, who was also editor of *Der Brenner*, among the leading progressive literary magazines of the time.

7| For a contemporary assessment of Loos's stature see, for example, Philip Lehmann, "Architektur von Menschen her," *Frankfurter Zeitung*, 8 February 1931, 17.

8| Nikolaus Pevsner, *Pioneers of the Modern Movement from William Morris to Walter Gropius* (London: Faber & Faber, 1936), 192.

9| Ludwig Münz and Gustav Künstler, *Der Architekt Adolf Loos: Darstellung seines Schaffens nach Werkgruppen/Chronologisches Werkverzeichnis* (Vienna and Munich: Schroll, 1964); Adolf Loos, *Sämtliche Schriften*, volume 1, ed. Franz Glück (Vienna: Herold, 1963). The second volume never appeared.

10| Adolf Loos, *Ins Leere gesprochen 1897–1900*, ed. Adolf Opel (Vienna: Prachner, 1981); Adolf Loos, *Trotzdem 1900–1930*, ed. Adolf Opel (Vienna: Prachner, 1982); Adolf Loos, *Gesammelte Schriften*, ed. Adolf Opel (Vienna: Lesethek, 2010).

11| Loos, *Trotzdem 1900–1930*, 82.

12| Ibid., 202–3.

13| See Burkhardt Rukschcio, "Ornament und Mythos," in Alfred Pfabigan, ed., *Ornament und Askese im Zeitgeist des Wien der Jahrhundertwende* (Vienna: Christian Brandstätter, 1985), 57–68.

14| Loos, "Ornement et crime," *Les cahiers d'aujourd'hui* 5 (June 1913), 47–56.

15| Loos, "Ornement et crime," *L'Esprit nouveau* 2 (November 1920): 159–168.

16| Loos, "Ornement et crime," *L'Architecture vivante* (Spring 1926): 8–30.

17| Loos, "Ornament und Verbrechen," *Frankfurter Zeitung*, 24 October 1929. The essay was subsequently reprinted in the *Prager Tagblatt* in November of the same year.

18| Adolf Opel, *Introduction to Ornament and Crime: Selected Essays*, 11.

19| Loos, *Trotzdem 1900–1930*, 51.

20| Lina Loos, *Das Buch ohne Titel: Erlebte Geschichten*, Adolf Opel and Herbert Schimek, eds. (Frankfurt and Berlin: Ullstein, 1986), 81.

21| Loos, *Trotzdem 1900–1930*, 152.

22| Ibid., 250.

23| Ibid., 126.

24| Oskar Kokoschka, *My Life*, trans. David Britt (New York: Macmillan, 1974), 36.

25| Loos, *Trotzdem 1900–1930*, 112.

26| Ibid., 100.

27| Ibid., 111.

Chapter 5

1| Carrie Paterson, ed., *Adolf Loos: A Private Portrait, by Claire Beck Loos* (Los Angeles: DoppelHouse Press, 2011), 24.

2| Elise Altmann-Loos and Claire were both Jewish; Lina Loos (née Obertimpfler) was not. Bessie Bruce, whom Loos sometimes represented as his wife, was also not Jewish, but they were never legally married.

3| Paterson, ed., *Adolf Loos*, 36.

4| Ibid., 37.

5| Ibid., 38.

6| Ibid., 93.

7| Ibid., 132–33.

8| Ibid., 138.

Chapter 6

1| Markus Kristan, *Ich warne Sie vor Josef Hoffmann: Adolf Loos und die Wiener Werkstätte* (Vienna: Metroverlag, 2014), 85–86.

2| Ibid., 89–90.

3| Ibid., 90.

4| Ibid., 90-91.

5| "Adolf Loos über die Wiener Werkstätte," *Neue Freie Presse*, 21 April 1927, 67, reprinted in Kristan, *Ich warne Sie vor Josef Hoffmann*, 56–57. This and all subsequent translations are mine.

6| "Offener Brief an Adolf Loos in der 'Neuen Freien Presse,'" *Wiener Allgemeine Zeitung*, 23 April 1927, 4, reprinted in Kristan, *Ich warne Sie vor Josef Hoffmann*, 58–59.

7| "Oberbaurat Josef Hoffmann über den Architekten Adolf Loos," *Neues Wiener Journal*, 2 July 1927, 4, reprinted in Kristan, *Ich warne Sie vor Josef Hoffmann*, 68–70.

8| Kristan, *Ich warne Sie vor Josef Hoffmann*, 121–22.

jaromír
funke
between
construction
and emotion

KOUDELKA
RETURNING

Theodor Pištěk
Petr Volf
Člověk a stroj Man and Machine

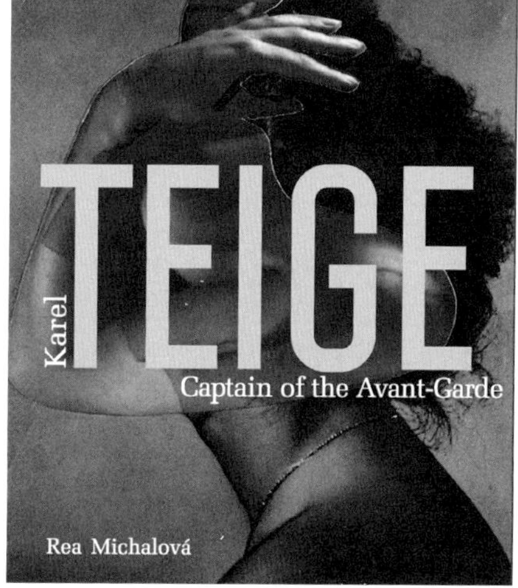
Karel
TEIGE
Captain of the Avant-Garde
Rea Michalová

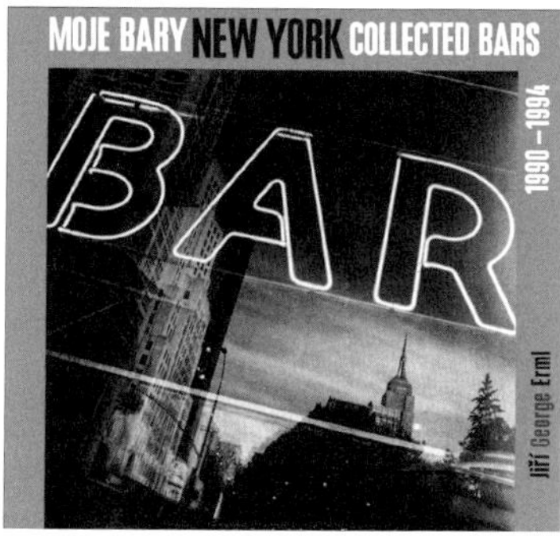
MOJE BARY NEW YORK COLLECTED BARS
BAR
1990 – 1994
Jiří George Erml

ADOLF LOOS ON TRIAL
Christopher Long

CIRCUS
SIDE SHOW
ANTONIN
KRATOCHVIL

Christopher Long – ESSAYS ON ADOLF LOOS

This book was published with assistance from the Martin S. Kermacy Endowment, School of Architecture at the University of Texas at Austin.

Cover photograph: Detail of the marble cladding of Adolf Loos' Goldman & Salatsch Building, Vienna, 1909–11. Photograph by Wolfgang Thaler

Graphic design and the picture editing:
| Jiří Příhoda
Publisher:
| Karel Kerlický – KANT 2019, Prague
www.kant-books.com

Print:
| Tiskárna PROTISK, s.r.o., České Budějovice, Czech Republic

ISBN: 978-80-7437-277-3